Bon voyage!

Jo Anne Wilson
Educational Consultant

Jacqueline Moase-Burke
Oakland Schools
Waterford, Michigan

Toni Theisen
Loveland Public Schools
Loveland, Colorado

HH **Heinle & Heinle Publishers**
A Division of Wadsworth, Inc.
Boston, Massachusetts 02116

CREDITS

The publication of *Bon voyage!* was directed by the members of the Heinle & Heinle School Publishing team:

Publisher: Stanley J. Galek
Editorial Director: Janet Dracksdorf
Marketing Manager: Elaine Uzan Leary
Production Editor: Pamela Warren
Developmental Editor: Margaret Potter

Also participating in the publication of this text were:

Editorial Production Manager: Elizabeth Holthaus
Assistant Editor: Mary McKeon
Manufacturing Coordinator: Jerry Christopher
Interior Design: Imageset Design
Interior Layout and Composition: Johnny D'Ziner
Cover Design: Imageset Design
Illustrations: Robin Swennes, Imageset Design

PHOTOGRAPHS

Stuart Cohen: pages 35 (all), 39, 50 (all), 56 (all), 57 (all).
W.D. Morgan: pages 10, 156 (top).
Alice Dawn: pages 59, 106, 131 (all), 156 (center, bottom).

Manufactured in the United States of America.

ISBN: 0-8384-4925-5

Heinle & Heinle Publishers is a division of Wadsworth, Inc.

10 9 8 7 6 5 4 3 2 1

DEDICATION

We dedicate this book to the special people in our lives, who have loved, supported, and encouraged us throughout this project:

- Vi Scharbat, Joe Scharbat and Sally Gorenflo, Ron Kramer and "Rudnicks"
- Mike Burke, the Moase family (Ken, Dale, Sue, Eric, Alex, Tina, Jacob, and Vanessa) and Myra Baughman
- Karl J. Weaver, Gail Bishop, and Jan Latona

ACKNOWLEDGEMENTS

We would like to acknowledge and thank our colleagues, Darlene Hindsley and Joyce Smetanka, who gave us their linguistic expertise.

REVIEWERS

In particular, we wish to thank the four teachers who reviewed our entire manuscript and gave us invaluable criticisms and suggestions.

Bob Abel
Roeper School
Bloomfield Hills, MI

Susan Malik
Swift Creek Middle School
Midlothian, VA

Yvette Parks
Norwood Public Schools
Norwood, MA

Patrick Raven
Foreign Language Department Chairman
School District of Waukesha
Waukesha, WI

CONTENTS

TO THE STUDENT 1

TO THE STUDENT

There are many languages in the world that people use to communicate with each other. In this book, you are about to explore one that is spoken in many parts of the world—FRENCH. You will learn not only some of the French language itself, but also information about the people who speak it and the countries where they live.

The lessons in **Bon voyage!**, called Elements, take you through the steps you would follow if you were preparing for and participating in a homestay as an exchange student in a French-speaking country. In fact, you will be working through these steps just as if you were really going! You will learn words and phrases that are important for communicating with the people you'll meet, and you will participate in activities that help you prepare for your trip and get the most out of your homestay experience when you get there.

As you begin, listen carefully to the sounds of the language. Then practice saying the words and phrases that you hear. Try them with your friends and family. Perhaps you can find an exchange student or someone in your community who speaks French, and you can practice with him or her! You'll also have an opportunity to write in a journal, which will help you remember the language as you practice your writing skills. In addition, you'll have an opportunity to use drawings and pictures as visual cues for remembering words and phrases.

Exploring a language that is different from your own is like learning a special code, and it can even help you understand your own language better. Learning any language is a process that takes place over an extended period of time. This book offers you an opportunity to start that process. As you progress through the Elements, have fun and explore! We really hope you'll have a **Bon voyage!**

LEARNING ABOUT HOMESTAY COUNTRIES, CITIES, AND LANGUAGES

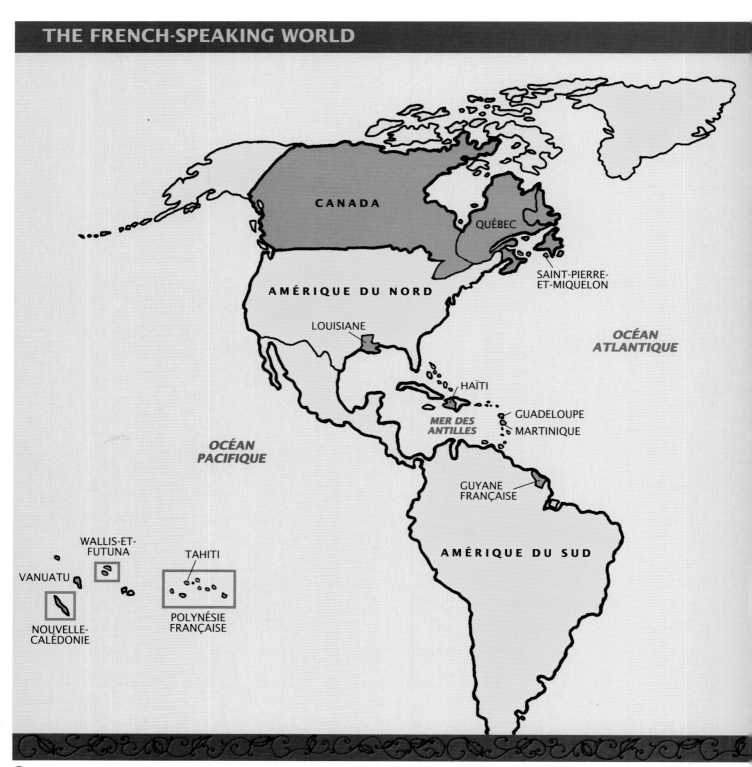

THE FRENCH-SPEAKING WORLD

CANADA

QUÉBEC

SAINT-PIERRE-ET-MIQUELON

AMÉRIQUE DU NORD

LOUISIANE

OCÉAN ATLANTIQUE

HAÏTI

GUADELOUPE

MARTINIQUE

MER DES ANTILLES

OCÉAN PACIFIQUE

GUYANE FRANÇAISE

AMÉRIQUE DU SUD

WALLIS-ET-FUTUNA

TAHITI

VANUATU

NOUVELLE-CALÉDONIE

POLYNÉSIE FRANÇAISE

PERSPECTIVE

The map below shows the many places around the world where French is spoken. In many, such as **Canada**, **Louisiane**, **Maroc**, **Égypte**, **Viêt-nam**, etc., French is not the only language spoken, but it is important. In this Element, you are going to learn about French-speaking countries. As you learn, think about one place in particular that you would like to visit. Why? Because this year, you are going on a homestay with a French-speaking family!

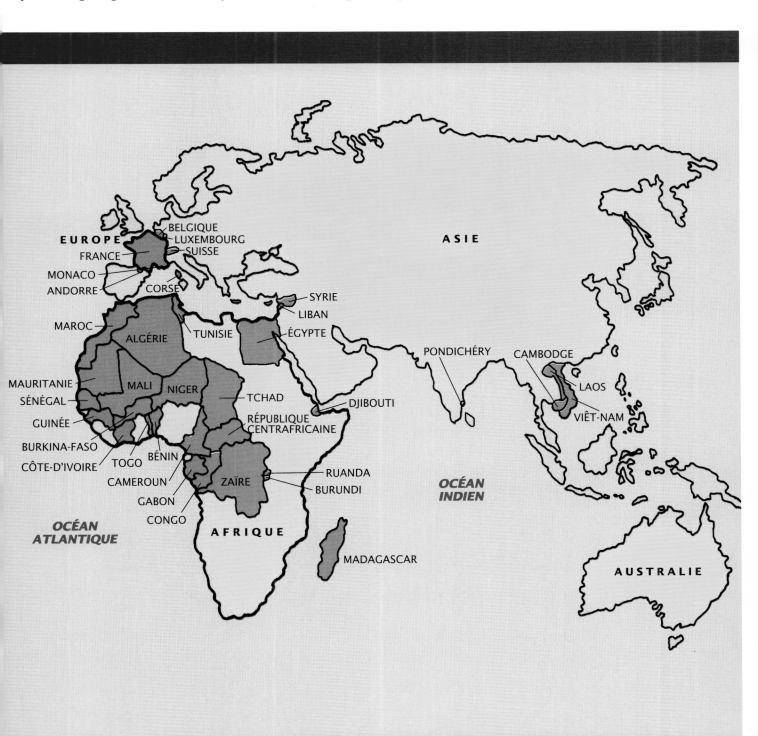

A. INTERNATIONAL YOUTH CONFERENCE

An international youth conference is taking place in your city. What a wonderful opportunity to meet young people from around the world! This is also a great time to get some first-hand information about a possible choice for your homestay country. At the conference, you decide to write down the names of all your new French-speaking friends and their countries. Find each country on your map of the world on pages 2 and 3.

Garçons	Pays/Région
Ahmed	Maroc
Alexandre	Belgique
Aliou	Bénin
Amadou	Niger
Bernard	Suisse
Dikembe	Zaïre
Jacques	France
Jean-Baptiste	Côte-d'Ivoire
Léopold	Sénégal
Mutimura	Djibouti
Paul	Tahiti
Pierre	Québec, Canada
Richard	Louisiane, États-Unis
Salim	Tunisie
Toussaint	Guadeloupe
Yambo	Mali

Filles	Pays/Région
Aïcha	Tunisie
Anne	France
Christine	Belgique
Claire	Suisse
Claudine	Luxembourg
Denise	Québec, Canada
Fatima	Burkina-Faso
Laïla	Algérie
Lamine	Togo
Magali	Madagascar
Marie-Léontine	Zaïre
Monique	Martinique
Nathalie	France
Nora	Maroc
Salah	Burundi
Stéphanie	Monaco
Zakia	Cameroun

B. MEETING NEW FRIENDS

At the youth conference registration table, you see all the name tags in different languages. This is your chance to meet students from the countries you'll be considering for your homestay. It's also your opportunity to practice using French to meet and greet someone. Look closely at the French name tags below.

Bonjour!

Je m'appelle *Jacques*
France

Pays/Région

International Youth Conference

Bonjour!

Je m'appelle *Zakia*

Pays/Région *Cameroun*

International Youth Conference

Bonjour!

Je m'appelle *Pierre*

Pays/Région *Québec, Canada*

International Youth Conference

Read the name tags. Then write the appropriate answer in each blank.

1. Which word on the name tag means *Hello?*_____

2. **Je m'appelle** means_____

3. Which words on the name tag mean *Country/Region?*_____

4. List the names of these three French-speaking students. _____

_____

5. There is one girl. What is her name?_____

6. List the names of the two boys. _____

7. List the three places these students come from. _____

_____

8. Locate these three countries on your map.

9. Who lives in **Québec, Canada?**_____

Now you are going to use three new French expressions—**Bonjour**, **Je m'appelle**, and **Enchanté(e)**—to meet and greet new French-speaking friends. Your teacher will review these expressions with you and tell you what to do.

C. YOUTH AMBASSADOR

All students who go on homestays become youth ambassadors for their countries. On your homestay, you'll be an ambassador for the United States. You'll be able to share your view of American life with your homestay family and new friends. Because the United States is a large country composed of people from many backgrounds, not everyone will have the same views you have.

1. *Individually:* Think about what your life is like in the United States. Which important aspects of your life would you like to share with your homestay family and new friends? Write them in your suitcase of ambassador information.

2. *In a small group*: Now share your own ideas with a small group of classmates. Listen to the other students express their ideas. Talk about what you will tell your host families about these things. If you like any of your classmates' ideas, you may add them to your own suitcase of ambassador information.

Favorite Foods

What's Important to Me

Favorite Pastimes

I am Proud of . . .

Favorite Customs

My Friends

D. FRANCE

Here is a map of **France**, the country in Europe (see your map of the French-speaking world) where the French language began. Maybe France will be your homestay destination. Let's look at some geographical terms in French.

A. How do French-speaking students write the following?

1. Atlantic Ocean _____

   _____

2. Mediterranean Sea_____

   _____

3. English Channel_____

   _____

B. Search the map to find the following information.

1. Circle the five major mountain regions on your map.

2. Name the river that flows through **Paris**. _____

3. Which very long river flows near the city of **Tours**? _____

4. Which river empties into the **Mer Méditerranée**?_____

5. France is bounded by _____ bodies of water. What do you think French students do when they go on vacation to one of these coastal areas? _____

   _____

6. Name three countries in **Europe** near **France** where French is spoken._____

   _____

7. Look at the map. Listen while your teacher names some of the geographic points of interest discussed above. When you hear a location, place your finger on that area of the map. Your teacher will give you the correct answer after naming each location. How many did you get right? Try doing the same with a partner.

E. CITIES IN FRANCE

Here are some important cities in France (**villes de France**). The homestay family you select may live in one of them. The first letter of the name of each city is on the map. Use the list below to complete the names on the map.

Paris	Nantes	Grenoble	Marseille	Rouen	Strasbourg
Bordeaux	Dijon	Lyon	Nice	Orléans	Tours

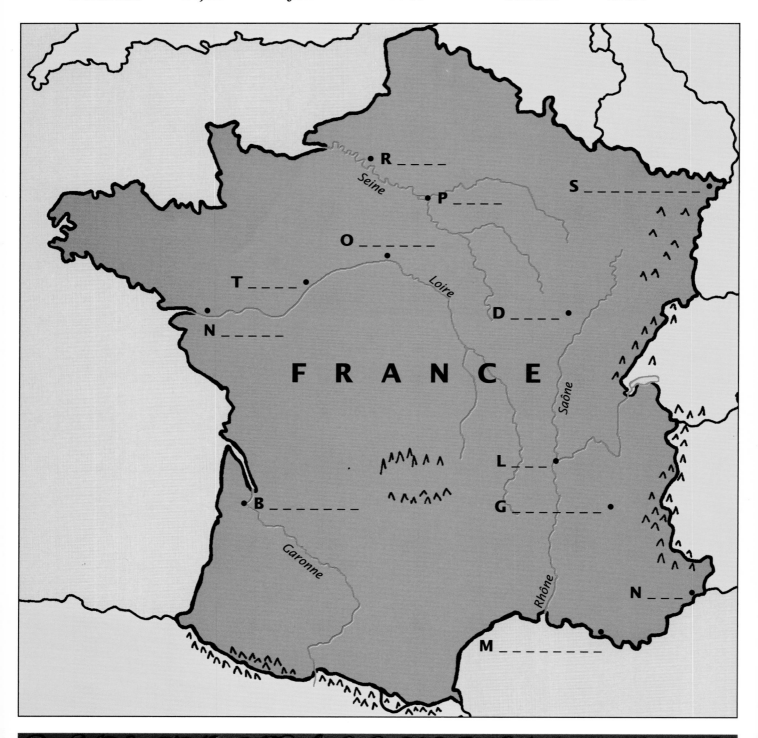

F. YOUR NEIGHBORS— CANADA AND THE CARIBBEAN

You might consider a homestay a little closer to home than France. Here is a map of Canada, the Caribbean, and part of South America (see your map of the French-speaking world). Let's look at some more geographical terms in French. These can be very useful in planning your visit.

 Canada has two official languages— English and French. Much of the country is English speaking. The highest concentration of French speakers is in **Québec** (where French is the only official language).

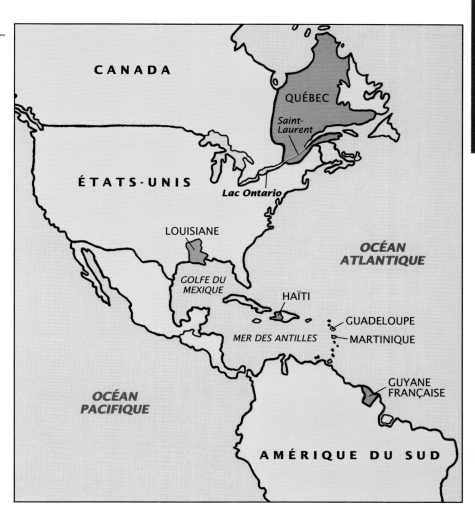

A. How do French-speaking students write the following?

1. Pacific Ocean _____

2. Atlantic Ocean _____

3. Gulf of Mexico _____

4. Caribbean Sea _____

B. Search the map to find the following information.

1. Name the area in the southern United States where French is spoken. _____

2. What is the French name for the river that runs from one of the Great Lakes to the **Océan Atlantique**? _____

3. What is the name of the French-speaking Canadian province that borders the northeast corner of the United States? _____

4. Which two French-speaking islands in the **Mer des Antilles** are close together? _____

_____

5. Which French-speaking country in the **Mer des Antilles** shares an island with a Spanish-speaking country? _____

6. Name the French-speaking region in **Amérique du Sud**. _____

_____

7. Look at the map. Listen while your teacher names some of the geographic points of interest discussed above. When you hear a location, place your finger on that area of the map. Your teacher will give you the correct answer after naming each location. How many did you get right? Try doing the same with a partner.

Château Frontenac and the Saint Lawrence River, Quebec City, Canada

G. AFRICA

Many people are surprised at the large number of French-speaking countries on the continent of Africa. You might consider a homestay in Africa. How exciting it would be to visit one of those wonderful countries! Look at the map of Africa. Here are some additional geographical terms in French.

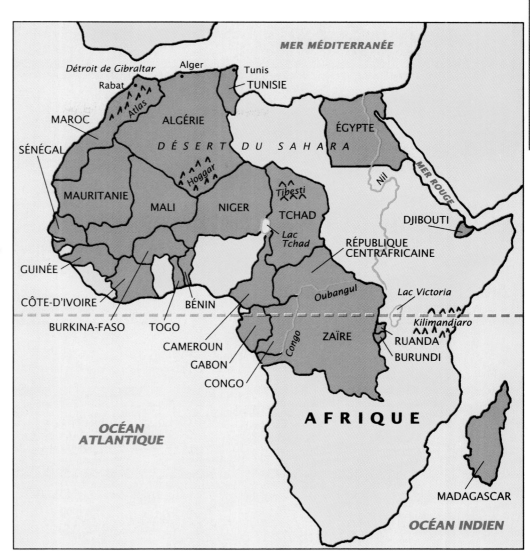

A. How do French-speaking students write the following?

1. Atlantic Ocean _____

2. Indian Ocean _____

3. Mediterranean Sea _____

4. Red Sea _____

5. Strait of Gibraltar _____

B. Search the map to find the following information.

1. Circle the major mountain ranges in northern Africa.

2. Which rivers run along the border of **Zaïre**? _____

_____

3. Trace the equator with your finger. What French-speaking countries does it cross?

_____

_____

4. Name the four northern-most countries in Africa where French is an important language.

_____

5. What country has a large lake with the same name as the country?_____

6. What is the name of the large desert in **Afrique**? _____

7. Look at the map. Listen while your teacher names some of the geographic points of interest discussed above. When you hear a location, place your finger on that area of the map. Your teacher will give you the correct answer after naming each location. How many did you get right? Try doing the same with a partner.

H. RECOGNIZING COUNTRIES AND CONTINENTS

You have learned about French-speaking countries around the world. Referring to your map on pages 2 and 3, review these countries. Find the continent where each country or region named below is located and write the letter code for that continent in the blank.

Amérique du Nord = **N**

Europe = **E**

Afrique = **A**

_____ 1. Québec, Canada

_____ 2. Sénégal

_____ 3. Martinique

_____ 4. Suisse

_____ 5. Maroc

_____ 6. Burkina-Faso

_____ 7. France

_____ 8. Cameroun

_____ 9. Belgique

_____ 10. Guadeloupe

_____ 11. Louisiane, États-Unis

_____ 12. Zaïre

I. FRENCH WORDS YOU KNOW: COGNATES

You've learned about the countries where French is spoken. Now you really need to focus on the language you will be learning. French is an exciting and interesting language. There are many French words that look like English words but are pronounced differently. These words, called cognates, may be spelled the same in both languages or a little differently. Here is a list of French words that last year's homestay students wrote for you. Let's see how many you know!

THINGS AND PEOPLE

l'abricot	la carotte	la gymnastique	l'océan	la science	la tomate
l'animal	la cathédrale	l'histoire	le parc	la soupe	le train
l'art	le chef	le hockey	le parent	le sport	le volley-ball
l'avenue	le chocolat	l'hôtel	la pizza	la statue	(le volley)
la banane	la classe	le jean	la poste	le steak	le voyage
le base-ball	la danse	la lettre	le pull-over	le taxi	le zoo
la biologie	la famille	le menu	la radio	le téléphone	
le boulevard	le football	le monument	le restaurant	la télévision	
la boutique	le fruit	la musique	la salade	le tennis	
le café	la géographie	la nature	le sandwich	la toilette	

DESCRIPTIONS

africain	bleu	grillé	intelligent	public
américain	délicieux	important	orange	violet

J. COGNATE CATEGORIES

Did you know a lot of the words in the list of cognates? Can you think of any others? Sort the words in the list into the following categories:

1. Sports

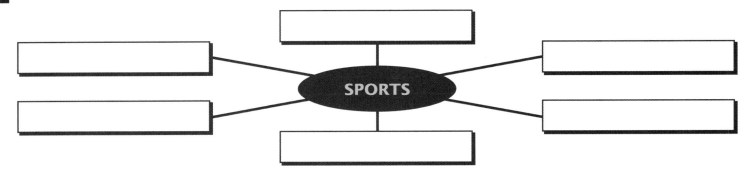

2. Food and drink

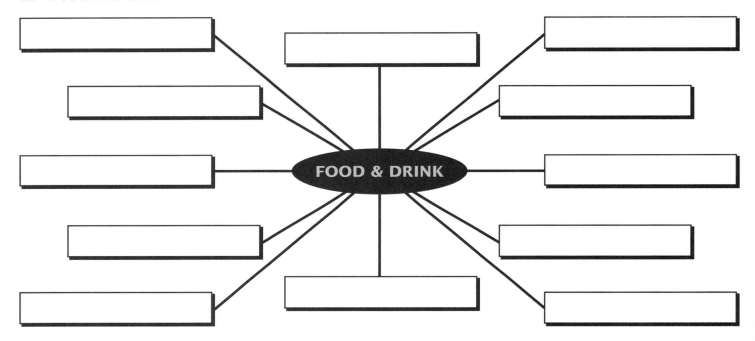

3. Modes of transportation _____

   _____

4. Colors _____

5. Create a category name in *English* for the following words from the list: **l'art, la biologie, la géographie, l'histoire.** _____

   _____

K. MY JOURNAL

You're ready to choose your homestay country. It helped to meet students who live in these countries, didn't it? You are going to keep a journal about your plans and your homestay. Select five to ten new French words you need to remember. Write those words in your journal under the heading **Mes mots**, which means *My words*. Also in your journal, include any new information you learned about French-speaking countries or continents. Write this information under **Nouveaux renseignements**, which means *New information*. Draw the flag and/or a map of your country under **Mon dessin**, which means *My drawing*.

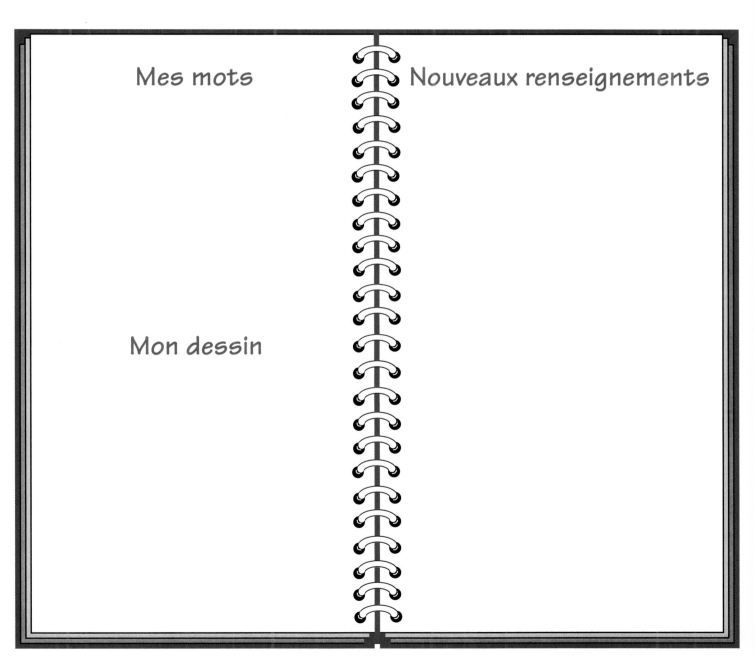

Mes mots

Nouveaux renseignements

Mon dessin

2 PACKING

PERSPECTIVE

Look at the picture of the suitcase to the right. What kinds of things do you think you'll be learning in this Element? Can you guess what the French words mean? How will learning about these things help you plan for your homestay?

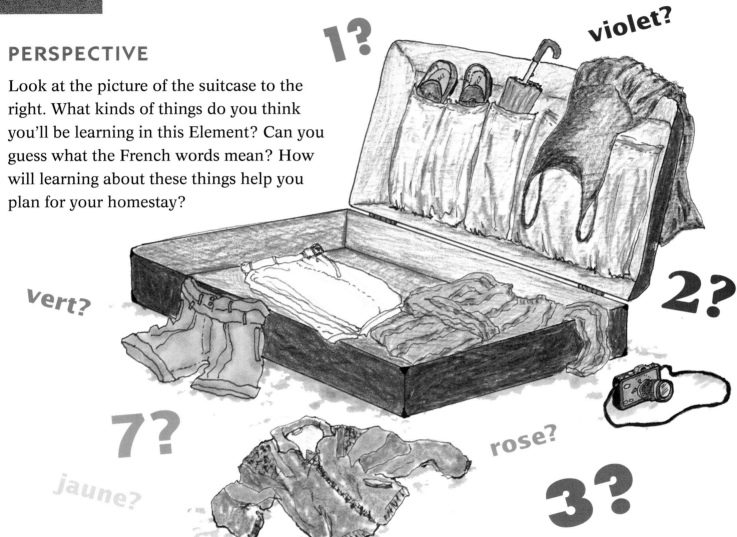

A. CLOTHING

By now you've selected a country for your homestay. It's never too early to think about the clothing you'll take on your trip. You want to have plenty of time to plan what you'll wear and to see if it will fit in your suitcase. On the next page are pictures of clothing and travel items you may want to pack for your trip. Listen carefully while your teacher says the words in French. Notice that the name of each item has another word in front of it. Both **le** and **la** are French words for *the*.

In French, you almost always include the equivalent of *the* when referring to the names of things. If you are talking about more than one, you use **les** (pronounced *lay*). **Le, la,** and **les** all mean *the*. Different, isn't it? But, with a little practice, you'll remember. To practice, look at the pictures again and say the French words with your teacher or a partner.

le tee-shirt

le jean

les chaussettes

la jupe

la robe

les chaussures

la ceinture

le peigne

la montre

le parapluie

le short

la brosse

le sweat-shirt

la brosse
à dents

la chemise

le pull-over

le sac à dos

le pantalon

le chemisier

le dentifrice

le blouson

Now, to remind yourself when to use **le**, **la**, and **les**, use the webs below to sort the items on page 17.

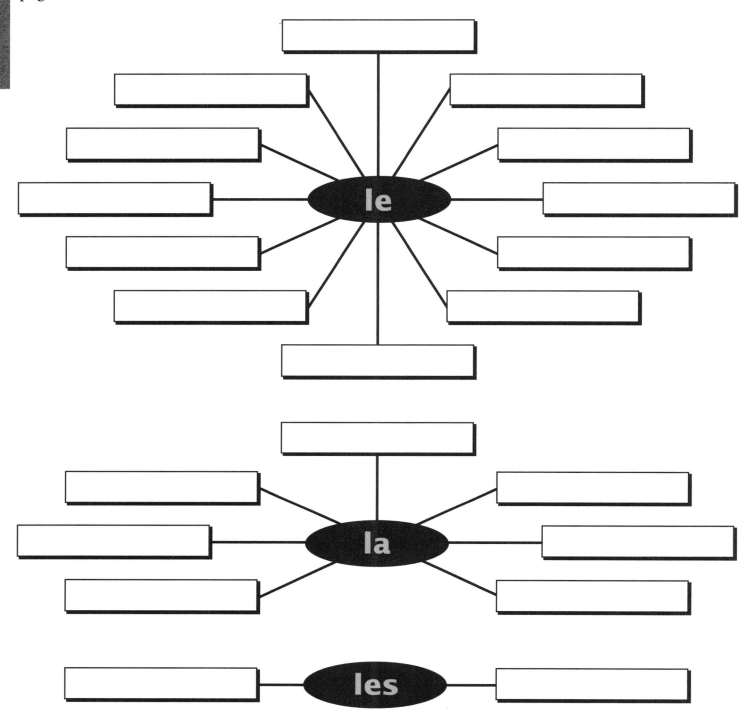

These words will be very helpful if you decide to do some shopping in your homestay country. Wouldn't it be great to buy a sweatshirt while you're there? Now you know exactly what to ask for in French.

B. NUMBERS

There are many reasons to learn French numbers (**les nombres**). You'll use numbers often during your homestay. Look at the French words for the numbers from 1 to 10. Count with your teacher.

1	**un**	3	**trois**	5	**cinq**	7	**sept**	9	**neuf**
2	**deux**	4	**quatre**	6	**six**	8	**huit**	10	**dix**

C. PACKING PRACTICE

You've learned the names of some clothing and travel items in French. On page 20 is a drawing of a large empty suitcase. Use this empty suitcase to practice packing. You'll need pictures from old magazines and catalogues or from the hand-out your teacher gives you. Or you may want to draw your own items. Follow these steps:

1. Cut out—or draw and cut out—pictures of clothing and travel items.
2. On the back of each item, write its French name.
3. Place the pictures on your desk so you can see all of them.
4. Listen as your teacher says the name of an item.
5. Place the picture of the item in your suitcase as you quietly repeat the name to yourself.
6. Check your progress with your teacher.

With a partner, take turns packing your suitcase.

1. Partner A names an item in French.
2. Partner B repeats the name of the item and places the picture of the item in the suitcase.
3. Partner A checks to see if Partner B packed the right thing.
4. When the suitcase is packed, change roles.
5. When you're sure you know the French names for all the items, paste the pictures in the suitcase.
6. Finally, label the pictures in the suitcase carefully in French.

D. HOW MANY ARE YOU TAKING?

One good way to practice French numbers is by talking about how many items you plan to pack for your homestay. You want to have enough of everything to last for the whole trip. Below is a list of some clothing and travel items you may need. Notice that there is an **s** on the end of most of the words. Both French and English add **s** when talking about more than one of an item. (Remember, though, that the **s** in French is not pronounced.) Follow these steps:

1. Listen as your teacher reads each item and quantity in French.
2. Write the corresponding numeral in the first blank after the item.
3. Check your answers as your teacher reads the numbers back to you.
4. Make any necessary corrections.
5. Finally, practice writing the French words for the numerals. Look at the numeral in the first blank. Write the French word for that numeral in the blank on the right as you quietly repeat the number to yourself.

Example:

chemises	*8*	huit
1. jean	_____	_____
2. chemisiers	_____	_____
3. chaussures	_____	_____
4. pantalons	_____	_____
5. pull-overs	_____	_____
6. robes	_____	_____
7. chaussettes	_____	_____
8. jupes	_____	_____
9. chemises	_____	_____
10. peignes	_____	_____

E. COLORS

What clothes to wear! How many clothes to take? You want to look terrific! What colors will be best? There are many reasons to learn the colors (**les couleurs**). If you decide to buy some clothes in your homestay country, you'll need to know how to ask for the colors you want. Look at the sweaters above and listen as your teacher says their colors in French. Then practice with a partner. In French, Partner A says the number of a sweater. Partner B then says the color of the sweater in French. When all the colors have been named, switch roles.

F. THE SUITCASE

In Activity A, you learned different ways French speakers say *the*. They also use different forms of many adjectives (words that describe people and things). This happens, for example, with colors. Look at the color words below. To know which form to use, take your cue from the French word for *the*. For some color words there are two choices. For others, there is only one.

LES COULEURS

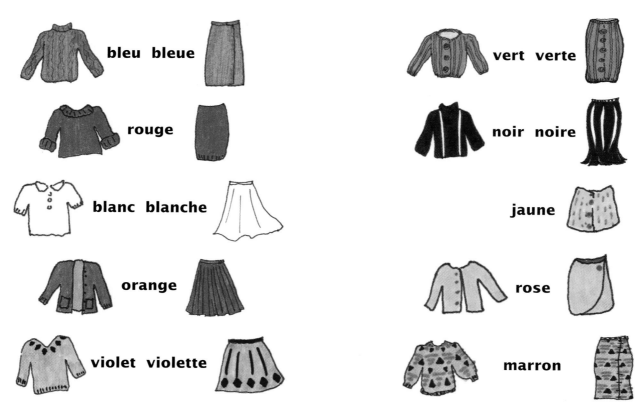

bleu bleue

rouge

blanc blanche

orange

violet violette

vert verte

noir noire

jaune

rose

marron

If there is only one choice, it is used with both **le** and **la**. When there are two choices, it works as follows:

- **"le"** words use the basic form of the color.
- **"la"** words use the **"e"** form of the color.

Here's an example of how you use the correct color word to describe an article of clothing.

le pull-over bleu   **la** jupe bleu**e**

The suitcase (**la valise**) below has been divided into two compartments, one labeled **Le** and one labeled **La**. Articles of clothing have been placed in the appropriate compartments. This makes it easy for you to select the correct form of the color word when there are two choices. If an item is in the **Le** compartment, choose the basic form of the color. If an item is in the **La** compartment, choose the form ending in **e**. If there is only one form of the color, it's easy—One form can be used for both. Choose a color for each item in the suitcase by writing the correct form of the color in the blank. Be sure to use each color at least once!

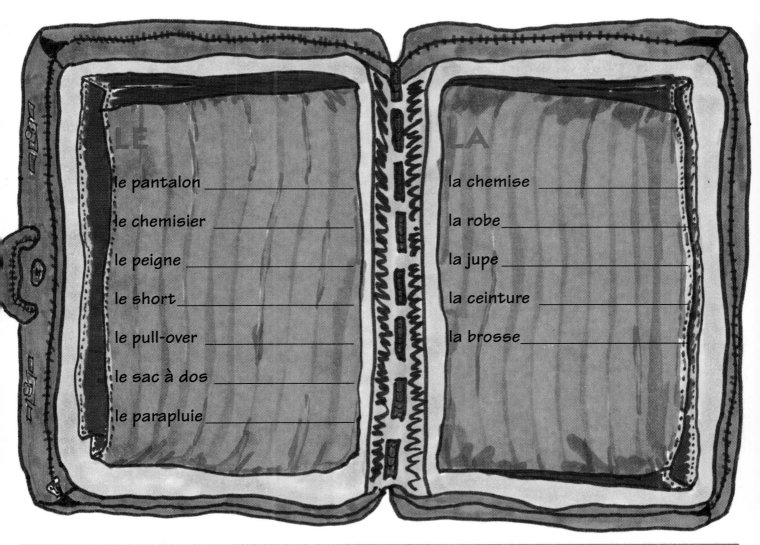

LE

le pantalon _____

le chemisier _____

le peigne _____

le short _____

le pull-over _____

le sac à dos _____

le parapluie _____

LA

la chemise _____

la robe _____

la jupe _____

la ceinture _____

la brosse _____

G. PACKING FOR YOUR TRIP

You have a lot of clothes, but you can take only a few. Here's a sample packing list. It names articles of clothing and travel items, and their colors. Circle the picture that corresponds to the description in the packing list.

 **Note** In Activity D you learned that French adds **s** to mean that there is more than one of an item. In the list below, you'll see that some *colors* have an **s** added because they describe more than one of an item. **Bonne chance!**

LISTE

1. jean bleu

2. tee-shirt blanc

3. blouson vert

4. chaussettes blanches

5. chemise rouge

6. chaussures marron

7. pull-over violet

8. pantalon noir

9. peigne rose

13. sac à dos bleu

10. brosse marron

14. brosse à dents verte

11. robe jaune

15. jupe orange

12. chemise orange

16. parapluie rouge

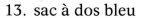  

Note Activity H on the next page gives practice in using a foreign-language dictionary. You may want to do that activity before you answer the following question.

Would you pack some things that aren't on the list above? To find out how to say them in French, ask your teacher or look in a dictionary. Then write them here.

_____ _____ _____

_____ _____ _____

_____ _____ _____

H. USING A DICTIONARY

When you use a foreign-language dictionary you will probably notice that it works differently from a regular English dictionary. To discover the differences and learn how to use a foreign-language dictionary, do the following:

Part 1. There are two sections in your French foreign-language dictionary: French–English and English–French. Put a check mark (√) to indicate the section you would use to look up each word.

	FRENCH–ENGLISH	ENGLISH–FRENCH
1. socks	_____	_____
2. pantalon	_____	_____
3. valise	_____	_____
4. jacket	_____	_____
5. chaussures	_____	_____
6. hat	_____	_____
7. chemise	_____	_____
8. jeans	_____	_____
9. blouson	_____	_____
10. chapeau	_____	_____

Part 2. Now answer these questions.

1. What are the two sections of a French foreign-language dictionary? _____

   _____

2. What can you learn about a noun in the French–English section besides its English

   translation? _____

3. How did you find the meaning of *chaussures*? _____

   _____

   _____

Part 3. With a partner, make a list of three English words and three French words that you know and give the list to your partner to look up in the dictionary.

I. MY JOURNAL

The airline allows you to take two pieces of luggage. You decide to take a suitcase (**valise**), and your backpack (**sac à dos**). You'll check **la valise** at the gate, but you'll keep **le sac à dos** with you. What will you put in your **valise** and what will you put in your **sac à dos**? (Remember to pack the most necessary items in **le sac à dos** in case the airline loses your suitcase.) In your journal, make a list of the items you need to take on your homestay. Decide how many and what colors of each item you'll need to pack. Then write each item on the journal page titled either **Valise** or **Sac à dos**, depending on where you'll pack it. Don't forget to use **le**, **la**, or **les** and the correct form of the color word.

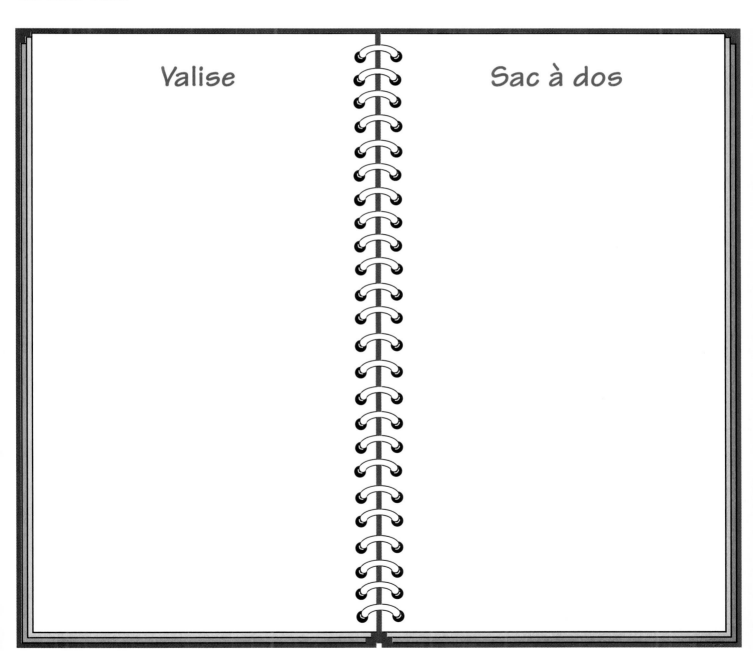

Valise

Sac à dos

3 TRIP PLANS

PERSPECTIVE

You've learned about homestay countries and thought about what to pack in your suitcase. Now it's time to make some other plans for your trip. One extremely important item that you'll need is a passport. In this Element, you'll fill out an application for a passport. You'll also learn more numbers and how to say months, days, and dates so you can schedule events.

A. L'ANNÉE SCOLAIRE (THE SCHOOL YEAR)

To set up a successful homestay trip, students, parents, and teachers need to begin to plan early. Homestay trips often take several months to organize. To plan your homestay adventure, you need to learn some important phrases in French.

An essential phrase for you to know is:

Comment dit-on _____ en français?   *How do you say _____ in French?*

The answer to this question is usually:

On dit _____.   *You say _____.*

For example, if you don't know the word for *month* in French, you will need to ask someone: **Comment dit-on *month* en français?** The person will then answer: **On dit *mois.***

Look at the months (**les mois**) written below. Circle any that you recognize. Many of them are cognates. (You learned about cognates in Element 1.) Read the months with your teacher. Here's the first page of a planning calendar for the school year (**l'année scolaire**). To practice the French spelling of the months, write them where they belong in the calendar. Begin with the first month of your school year. In French, you do not capitalize the names of months.

mai   octobre   mars   septembre   juillet   décembre
février   avril   novembre   août   janvier   juin

l'année scolaire

_____   _____

_____   _____

_____   _____

_____   _____

_____   _____

_____   _____

B. MON ANNIVERSAIRE (MY BIRTHDAY)

Now that you know the twelve months (**les douze mois**) of the year, you can identify the month of your birthday. *My birthday* in French is **mon anniversaire**. Look at the French word for *birthday*. Does it look like a word you know in English? That's right! Your birthday is the anniversary of your date of birth!

Write the **mois** of your **anniversaire** here. _____

C. LES ENQUÊTES (SURVEYS)

Surveys are a good way to get information. To find out when your classmates and other people have birthdays, complete the following two **enquêtes.** Then report your findings to the class. Remember to use only French for these **enquêtes.**

1. *Survey your classmates.* Circulate around the room and ask all the students in the class: **En quel mois est ton anniversaire?** (*In what month is your birthday?*) Each time a person answers, write his or her initials next to the month. Ready? (**Prêt[e]?**) Let's go! (**Allons-y!**)

En quel mois est ton anniversaire?		
janvier	mai	septembre
février	juin	octobre
mars	juillet	novembre
avril	août	décembre

Recording your data:

Which **mois** has the most **anniversaires?** _____

Which **mois** has the fewest **anniversaires?** _____

2. *Survey some other people.* Find five other people to interview. Write their names in the boxes labeled **Nom** (*Name*) below. Ask them when their birthday is. Write the month of each person's birthday in French in the second column, next to his or her name.

Nom	Anniversaire
1.	
2.	
3.	
4.	
5.	

D. LES JOURS DE LA SEMAINE (DAYS OF THE WEEK)

Look at the blank calendar below. Write the name of the current month in the space at the top of the calendar. To complete the calendar, what else do you need? You're right—you need days of the week and dates. **Comment dit-on** *day* **en français? On dit** *jour.*

French speakers think of the week as beginning with Monday (**lundi**) and ending with the weekend, Saturday (**samedi**) and Sunday (**dimanche**).

The days of the week (**les jours de la semaine**) are not capitalized in French. Practice saying the days of the week. Your teacher will get you started.

lundi   mardi   mercredi   jeudi   vendredi   samedi   dimanche

Look at the calendar again. In the seven spaces below the name of the month, fill in the **jours de la semaine**. Remember to begin with **lundi** on the left.

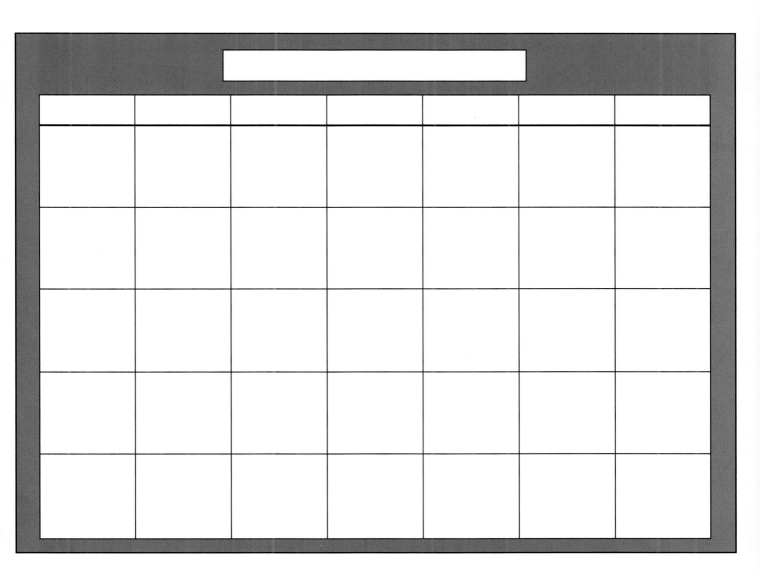

E. LES NOMBRES (NUMBERS)

Knowing the months of the year and days of the week is important to your homestay preparations. Look again at the calendar in Activity D on page 31. You have already filled in the name of this month and the days of the week. To use the calendar, you need the dates. Complete the calendar on page 31 for the current month by beginning with 1 on the correct day of the week. You've already learned the numbers from 1 to 10. Count quietly to yourself in French as you put the numerals 1 to 10 in the upper-left corner of the appropriate squares for this month. Stop at 10.

To complete your calendar, you need to become familiar with the numbers from 11 to 31. Here they are:

Les nombres de 11 à 31

		20	**vingt**	30	**trente**
11	**onze**	21	**vingt et un**	31	**trente et un**
12	**douze**	22	**vingt-deux**		
13	**treize**	23	**vingt-trois**		
14	**quatorze**	24	**vingt-quatre**		
15	**quinze**	25	**vingt-cinq**		
16	**seize**	26	**vingt-six**		
17	**dix-sept**	27	**vingt-sept**		
18	**dix-huit**	28	**vingt-huit**		
19	**dix-neuf**	29	**vingt-neuf**		

Together with your teacher and classmates, say the **nombres**. Then write the **nombres** you need into your calendar, saying them softly to yourself. Now, your calendar is complete and you're ready to plan important dates for your homestay.

F. LA DATE (THE DATE)

In addition to the date (**la date**) on a calendar, you will see dates in newspapers, magazines, advertisements for events, TV listings, and on tickets. Examine **les dates** below, which appear on items you're likely to see in your homestay country.

le 14 juillet   13/4   31/1

le 2 avril   24/12   le 7 septembre

What do you notice about the way dates are shown in French-speaking countries? That's exactly right! The month and day are reversed from the way we show them in the United States. Here's a little practice to sharpen your eye for the way dates are written in French-speaking countries.

Match the French and English dates below. Put the letter of the French date in the blank next to the corresponding date in English. The first one is done for you.

A. le 15 février   1. _____ July 25

B. le 25 décembre   2. _____ April 1

C. le 12 mars   3. _____ December 25

D. le 1er mai   4. _____ March 12

E. le 25 juillet   5. _____ September 15

F. le 12 octobre   6. _____ October 12

G. le 1er avril   7. _____ May 1

H. le 15 septembre   8. __A__ February 15

Note   When French speakers talk about the first of the month or the first day of each month, they use the words **le premier** or **le premier jour de**. For example:

le premier janvier   *the first of January*
le premier jour de janvier   *the first day of January*

Study the dates above. How do French speakers write **premier** as a numeral?_____

G. LA DATE EN CHIFFRES (THE DATE IN NUMERALS)

In Activity F you learned about using words to write dates in French. Sometimes you will see a date written entirely in numerals (**en chiffres**). When numerals are used to write a date in French-speaking countries, they are written in the same order as dates using words: day/month. So May 3 is written in French as **3/5** (the third day of the fifth month). This same date could be written as **le 3 mai.** Remember these differences when you make plans with your French-speaking friends. You wouldn't want to miss an important event, would you? Look at the dates below. They are written the way you will see them in your homestay country.

10/2	**le 10 février**
6/4	**le 6 avril**
12/9	**le 12 septembre**

Have you figured out the pattern?

Write your birthday in numerals as you would write it in a French-speaking country. _____

Then write out your birthday using words. _____

Practicing dates will help you prepare for your homestay experience. Why not practice by planning when you'll make payments for your homestay? Payments are due every two months from the date of the first payment. Look at the example below. The first column shows the date when the first payment of money for the trip is due. Calculate the date of your next payment. Write this date in both numerals and words.

Example: le 13 mai (+ 2 mois = le 13 juillet)   *13/7   le treize juillet*

1. le 10 février   _____   _____

2. le 1er mars   _____   _____

3. le 7 juillet   _____   _____

4. le 30 octobre   _____   _____

5. le 29 août   _____   _____

6. le 25 avril   _____   _____

7. le 13 juin   _____   _____

When you finish, check your answers with the rest of the class. Your teacher will help you.

H. DEUX PASSEPORTS
(TWO PASSPORTS)

You'll need to get a passport (**un passeport**) to travel to most other countries. Review the information in Jennifer Johnson's **passeport**.

Now look at the French **passeport** belonging to François Laroche. Compare the two **passeports**. Do you see any of the same information?

Compare the information presented in Jennifer's and François' **passeports**. Then answer the questions below.

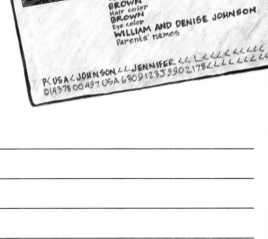

French actually has two words for *brown*. **Marron** is used for clothing, furniture, etc. But for hair and eye color, the more common word is **brun(e)**.

1. **Nom de famille** de Jennifer _____
   de François _____

2. **Date de naissance** de Jennifer _____
   de François _____

3. **Téléphone** de Jennifer _____
   de François _____

4. **Couleur des yeux** de Jennifer _____
   de François _____

5. **Adresse** de Jennifer _____
   de François _____

Circle the best response for each of these passport questions.

1. Date de naissance?

   a. Laroche   b. 1.44.37.64.36   c. Paris, France   d. 15/3/82

2. Nom de famille?

   a. Johnson   b. Jennifer   c. 303-667-9014   d. 1.44.37.64.36

3. Téléphone?

   a. Johnson   b. Jennifer   c. 303-667-9014   d. 7/7/83

4. Couleur des cheveux?

   a. Laroche   b. bruns   c. 7/7/83   d. François

5. Adresse?

   a. 1.44.37.64.36   b. Laroche   c. 39, avenue Jean-Moulin d. 15/3/82

I. DEMANDE DE PASSEPORT (PASSPORT APPLICATION)

Part 1. Now it's time to apply for your passport. Your teacher will give you a copy of the application form. Look at Jennifer's and François' **passeports** if you need help.

Part 2. When you land at the airport in your homestay country, your first stop will be to have your passport checked. To help you get ready, your teacher will give you the forms to make a **passeport** for classroom practice. After you make it, practice presenting it to the immigration officer. Your teacher will show you what to do.

J. MON JOURNAL (MY JOURNAL)

Select five to ten new French words from Element 3 that you need to remember. Write them under **Mes mots**. Don't forget to record new information in your journal under **Nouveaux renseignements.**

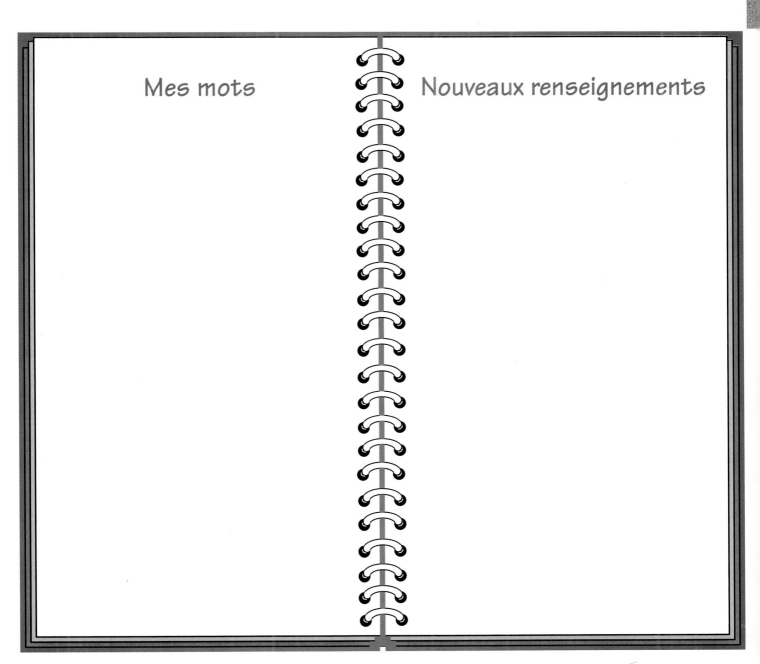

Mes mots

Nouveaux renseignements

TRAVEL DETAILS

PERSPECTIVE

Your trip is beginning to take shape. With your **passeport** in hand and your knowledge about your host country, you'll soon be ready. In this Element, you'll begin to prepare information about yourself that will be given to your host family before your visit. In addition, you will learn how to tell time and how to complete a luggage tag. **Prêt(e)? Allons-y!**

A. FICHE DE RENSEIGNEMENTS PERSONNELS

Preparations for your homestay are progressing very well! You're learning about the country you'll visit and how to say some essential words and phrases in French. Remember—if you need to know how to say something in French, ask: **Comment dit-on _____ en français?** *(How do you say _____ in French?)* It will be a useful question when you are with your host family.

Now it's time to complete the **Fiche de renseignements personnels** *(Personal Information Form)*. It is your way of introducing yourself to your host family and helping them get to know you. On the next page is a copy of the **Fiche de renseignements personnels** that Jennifer Johnson completed last year. It has two parts. Look at the first part. Circle the words that are new to you. Can you guess what they mean? Do you recognize some words from the passport activity in Element 3? If you need help with new words, ask your teacher.

RENSEIGNEMENTS PERSONNELS

Nom de famille _____Johnson_____

Prénom _____Jennifer_____

Âge _____12 ans_____

Adresse _____3576 Applegate Street_____
_____Loveland, Colorado 80537 U.S.A._____
_____

Téléphone _____303-667-9014_____

Mon école _____Loveland Middle School_____

Mon professeur de français s'appelle _____Mme Kramer_____

Mes parents _____William et Denise Johnson_____

J'ai ___1___ frère(s) ___2___ sœur(s)

J'ai

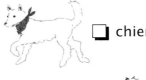 ☐ chien

 ☑ chat

 ☐ poisson

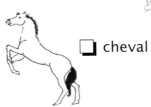 ☐ cheval

 ☑ oiseau

In the second part, Jennifer indicated her favorite activities (**activités préférées**) and favorite sports (**sports préférés**) so that her host family would know about her favorite pastimes. To do this, Jennifer used two French expressions that you will also need to use: **J'aime** (*I like*) and **Je n'aime pas** (*I don't like*). Review Jennifer's favorite pastimes. The pictures next to the words will help you understand their meanings.

Mes activités préférées (*J'aime* = √; *Je n'aime pas* = X)

- ☒ danser
- ☑ aller au cinéma
- ☑ manger au restaurant
- ☑ aller au parc
- ☑ écouter de la musique
- ☒ faire des courses
- ☑ faire de la photo
- ☒ lire
- ☑ parler avec mes amis
- ☑ regarder la télé
- ☑ parler au téléphone
- ☑ voyager

Mes sports préférés (*J'aime* = √; *Je n'aime pas* = X)

- ☐ l'aviation
- ☑ le football
- ☐ le basket
- ☐ la gymnastique
- ☒ le base-ball
- ☐ le karaté
- ☐ le vélo
- ☑ la natation
- ☑ le ski
- ☐ le tennis
- ☐ le ski nautique
- ☒ le volley

B. REMPLIR LA FICHE

Jennifer Johnson's **Fiche de renseignements personnels** gave the host family information about her before she arrived. Now, you need to fill out a form for your own homestay. Remember that the phrases **J'aime** and **Je n'aime pas** mean *I like* and *I don't like.* You'll use them often as you travel. For now, you'll be noting which **activités** and **sports** you like or don't like. Look at the pictures illustrating each activity or sport. These pictures give clues to the meaning of the words and phrases. Please start with the first section, **Renseignements personnels. Prêt(e)? Allons-y!**

RENSEIGNEMENTS PERSONNELS

Nom de famille _____ Prénom _____ Âge _____

Adresse _____ Téléphone _____

Mon école _____ Mon professeur de français _____

Mes parents _____ J'ai _____ frère(s) _____ sœur(s)

J'ai 🐕 ☐ chien   🐾 ☐ chat   🐴 ☐ cheval   🐦 ☐ oiseau   🐟 ☐ poisson

Mes activités préférées (*J'aime* = √; *Je n'aime pas* = X)

☐ danser

☐ aller au cinéma

☐ manger au restaurant

☐ aller au parc

☐ écouter de la musique

☐ faire des courses

☐ faire de la photo

☐ lire

☐ parler avec mes amis

☐ regarder la télé

☐ parler au téléphone

☐ voyager

Mes sports préférés (*J'aime* = √; *Je n'aime pas* = X)

☐ l'aviation

☐ le football

☐ le basket

☐ la gymnastique

☐ le base-ball

☐ le karaté

☐ le vélo

☐ la natation

☐ le ski

☐ le tennis

☐ le ski nautique

☐ le volley

C. LA PRÉPARATION DU VOYAGE

In Element 3, you learned the days of the week (**les jours de la semaine**). Here is a page from Jennifer's planning calendar from last year. Review **les jours** and the things she did. As you review, think about your own trip and how you will organize your own list of travel preparations.

JUIN

lundi, le 12 juin
Prepare album of family and friends

mardi, le 13 juin
Purchase traveler's checks

mercredi, le 14 juin
Buy travel journal

jeudi, le 15 juin
Buy a gift for host family

vendredi, le 16 juin
Record addresses of family and friends

samedi, le 17 juin
Pack suitcase

dimanche, le 18 juin
Say good-bye to friends

After reviewing Jennifer's calendar, read the statements below. Pay careful attention to the **jours.** Decide if each statement is true (**vrai**) or false (**faux**). Check (√) the correct answer.

		vrai	faux
1.	Jennifer packed her suitcase on Saturday.	_____	_____
2.	She bought a gift for her host family on Monday.	_____	_____
3.	Jennifer purchased traveler's checks on Thursday.	_____	_____
4.	She said good-bye to friends on Sunday.	_____	_____
5.	She bought her travel journal on Wednesday.	_____	_____
6.	Jennifer traveled in July.	_____	_____

D. L'ORGANISATION DE LA SEMAINE

Look at the notes below. Each drawing should jog your memory about something you need to do before you leave. Decide on which day of the week (**jour de la semaine**) you have time for each task. Write the French word for that day next to **jour** on each note. You also have two blank notes for additional tasks. If you wish to use these extra notes, put a picture and a related word on each. Use your time wisely. Plan to complete at least one task per day, but don't list them all for the same day.

E. COMPARAISON AVEC UN(E) AMI(E)

You now have your week's schedule of things to do. If you coordinate your efforts with a friend, you can save time and energy. Working with a partner, compare schedules. Partner A reads the activity from the grid below. Partner B responds by telling the **jour** that he or she will complete the task. Check the **jour** you hear for each task. Reverse roles.

ACTIVITÉ	lundi	mardi	mercredi	jeudi	vendredi	samedi	dimanche
buy travel journal							
pack suitcase							
prepare family photo album							
say good-bye to friends							
record family/friends addresses							
buy traveler's checks							
buy gift for host family							

When you're done, look at the two grids. Did both of you plan things for the same **jour**? If not, check (√) **non** _____ . If yes, check (√) **oui** _____ . Decide how you will share the responsibility for getting these things done.

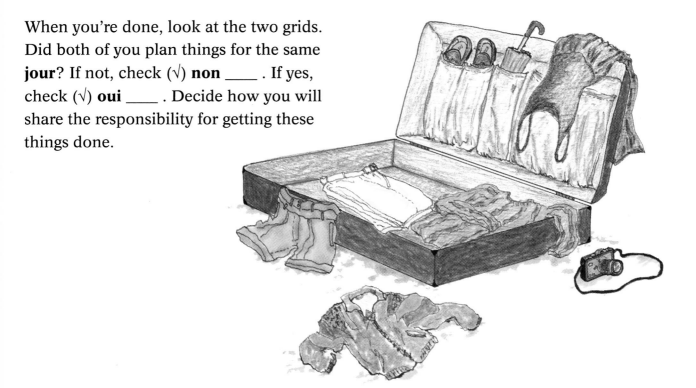

F. QUELLE HEURE EST-IL?

Your trip will involve many scheduled activities. Understanding how time is expressed in French will be crucial. You already know the numbers from 1 to 31. Quietly say the numbers from 1 to 12 as a review. When you want to say *It's two o'clock* in French, you say **Il est deux heures.** Look at the clocks below and say the times shown. Remember to begin with **Il est.** Watch out for *one o'clock*. It's a little different.

 Twelve o'clock can mean either *It's noon* or *It's midnight*. You'll want to be able to express the difference.

Comment dit-on *It's noon* **en français?**   **On dit:** *Il est midi.*
Comment dit-on *It's midnight* **en français?**   **On dit:** *Il est minuit.*

  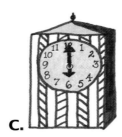 

A.   B.   C.   D.

E.   F.   G.   H.

Using your skill with numbers, match the times on the clocks above with the words below. Put the letter of the clock in the blank that indicates the time shown on the clock.

1. _____ Il est six heures.   5. _____ Il est deux heures.

2. _____ Il est onze heures.   6. _____ Il est dix heures.

3. _____ Il est cinq heures.   7. _____ Il est minuit.

4. _____ Il est une heure.   8. _____ Il est midi.

Easy, isn't it? **C'est facile, non?**

How do you write *It's one o'clock*? _____

How is this time different from the other times? _____

G. UNE HORLOGE

Now let's make a clock (**une horloge**). To do this project you will need:

- a small paper plate
- a piece of cardboard to make the hands of the clock
- a fastener
- crayons or markers to write numbers
- scissors

Instructions

1. Cut out two clock hands. Make one longer than the other.
2. Punch holes in the center of the plate and near the end of each hand.
3. Attach the two hands to the plate with a fastener.
4. Write the numbers on the clock face.
5. Decorate the clock face.

You are now ready for clock activities. First, your teacher will say a time of day in French. Set your clock by moving the hands to show the time. Hold your clock up as soon as you've set it.

Next, work with a partner. Each of you creates a list of five different on-the-hour times. Partner A says his or her times to Partner B. Partner B sets his or her clock to show the correct times. Reverse roles. Each of you can keep a tally of the number of correct responses. Keep your clock because you will use it again as you study time in more detail.

H. À QUELLE HEURE?

Now you've learned how to say what time it is. For example, *It's five o'clock* = **Il est cinq heures.**
To say *at what time* (**à quelle heure**) something happens, you just change the beginning: *at five o'clock* = **à cinq heures**. Look at this example:

Allons-y! **Il est cinq heures.**   *Let's go! It's five o'clock.*
J'aime regarder la télé **à cinq heures.**   *I like to watch TV at five o'clock.*

To specify *at noon* and *at midnight*, use **à midi** or **à minuit**.
To ask *At what time?*, say **À quelle heure?**

In this exercise, you'll tell at what time something happens. Below are some activities scheduled during your homestay. Review the schedule sheet. Then listen as your teacher tells the starting time for each activity. Place a check mark (√) in the box of the announced time.

ACTIVITÉ	1:00	2:00	3:00	4:00	5:00	6:00	7:00	8:00	9:00	10:00	11:00	12:00
faire des courses												
aller au concert												
aller au musée												
aller au match de football												
manger												
aller à l'école												
jouer au tennis												
parler au téléphone												
aller au cinéma												

I. L'ÉTIQUETTE À BAGAGES

You will need a luggage tag (**étiquette à bagages**) for your suitcase. In your homestay country you'll be asked to fill out a different tag for the return trip. It will look like this. Complete the **étiquette** with your **renseignements personnels**.

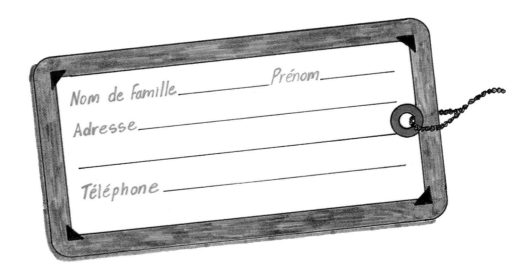

J. MON JOURNAL

Record new information in your journal. Include facts about yourself that you want your host family to know. Remember to use **J'aime** and **Je n'aime pas** to describe your favorite **activités** and **sports.** Write this information under **Nouveaux renseignements**. Select five to ten new French words from Element 4 that you need to remember. Write these words under **Mes mots.**

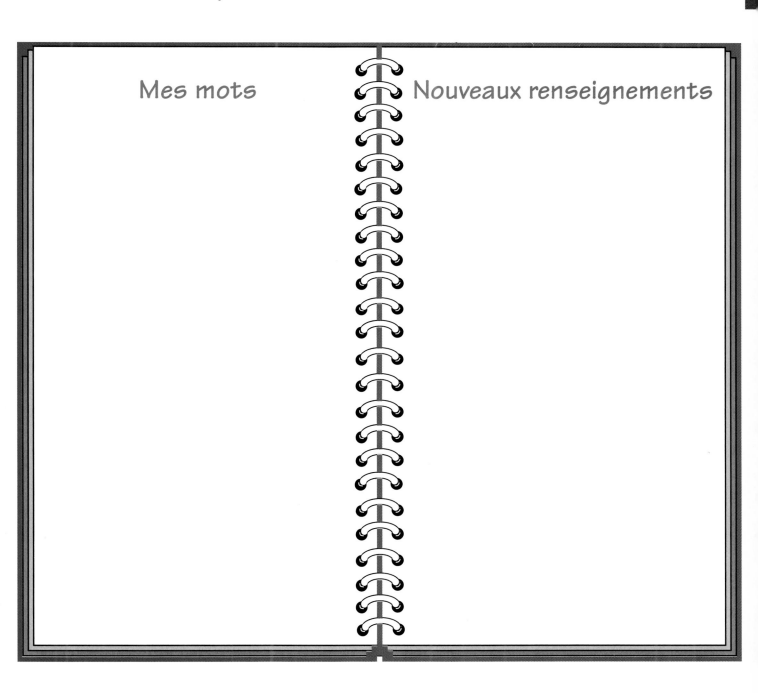

Mes mots

Nouveaux renseignements

5

EXCHANGING LETTERS WITH YOUR HOST FAMILY

PERSPECTIVE

Your passport has arrived! It's time to select your host family and begin writing to them. Exchanging letters and pictures will help you get acquainted.

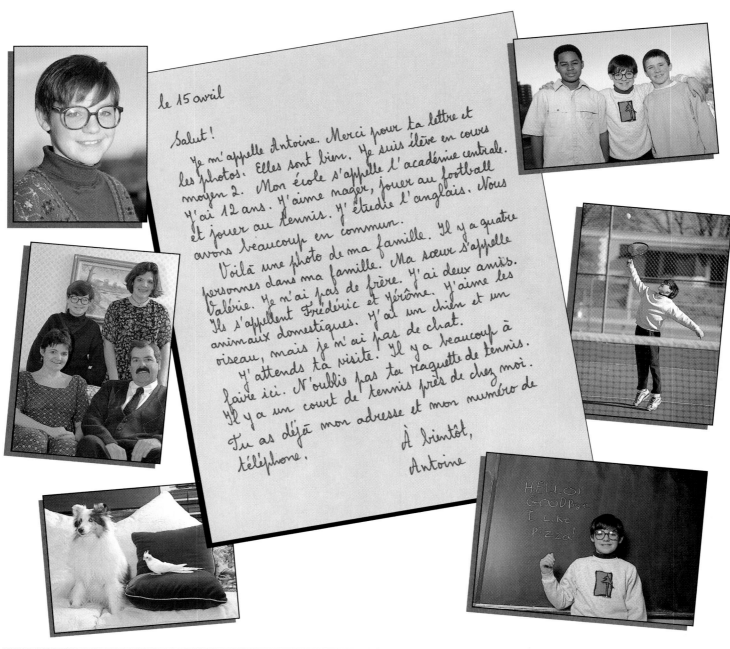

le 15 avril

Salut!

Je m'appelle Antoine. Merci pour ta lettre et les photos. Elles sont bien. Je suis élève en cours moyen 2. Mon école s'appelle l'académie centrale. J'ai 12 ans. J'aime nager, jouer au football et jouer au tennis. J'étudie l'anglais. Nous avons beaucoup en commun.

Voilà une photo de ma famille. Il y a quatre personnes dans ma famille. Ma sœur s'appelle Valérie. Je n'ai pas de frère. J'ai deux amis. Ils s'appellent Frédéric et Jérôme. J'aime les animaux domestiques. J'ai un chien et un oiseau, mais je n'ai pas de chat.

J'attends ta visite. Il y a beaucoup à faire ici. N'oublie pas ta raquette de tennis. Il y a un court de tennis près de chez moi. Tu as déjà mon adresse et mon numéro de téléphone.

À bientôt,
Antoine

A. LES NOMBRES DE 10 À 1.000

The organization in charge of the homestay program will send you a list of host families. You will select your homestay family from this list. The list will also give each family's address and telephone number (**numéro de téléphone**). These will be very important for you to remember, because they will be your **adresse** and **numéro de téléphone** for the duration of your homestay!

 Notice that the French use two different words for *number*. **Nombre** refers to a quantity or to the idea, while **numéro** means the number given to a specific thing to identify it (such as a **numéro de téléphone**).

To understand and give your homestay **adresse** and **numéro de téléphone** in French, you need to know **les nombres** from 10 to 1,000.

Look at the numbers below. Which ones do you already know? Count quietly to yourself as your teacher counts aloud. Count by tens from 10 to 100, starting with **dix**. Then, starting with **cent**, continue counting by hundreds from 100 to 1,000.

10	**dix**	100	**cent**
20	**vingt**	200	**deux cents**
30	**trente**	300	**trois cents**
40	**quarante**	400	**quatre cents**
50	**cinquante**	500	**cinq cents**
60	**soixante**	600	**six cents**
70	**soixante-dix**	700	**sept cents**
80	**quatre-vingts**	800	**huit cents**
90	**quatre-vingt-dix**	900	**neuf cents**
100	**cent**	1.000	**mille**

 Look at the way French speakers write the numeral for one thousand. In French, one thousand is sometimes written with a period (1.000) and sometimes with a space (1 000). Both forms are understood in French-speaking countries.

Practice counting by tens or hundreds, starting from 10, 12, or 15. Your teacher will tell you what to do.

Now that you know these higher numbers, you're ready to learn your new **adresse** and **numéro de téléphone.**

B. L'ADRESSE ET LE NUMÉRO DE TÉLÉPHONE DE MA FAMILLE

You're ready to make your homestay selection. Here is the list of host families. They live in several different French-speaking countries. In Element 1, there are maps to help you locate these countries. Now, select a host family and country for your homestay. Choose your family from the list. Put a check mark (√) next to your choice.

❏ **M. et Mme Abdul**
14, avenue Mulay Ismaïl
Rabat, Maroc
(212) 7.75.30.50

❏ **M. et Mme Gie**
3, place Louis XIV
Grenoble, France
(33) 76.50.60.70

❏ **M. et Mme Artiste**
60, avenue Bourguiba
Kairouan, Tunisie
(216) 7.1.49.07

❏ **M. et Mme Guillaume**
20, boulevard du 1066
Paris, France
(33) 1.46.70.20.20

❏ **M. et Mme Chinon**
3, rue Jeanne-d'Arc
Nice, France
(33) 93.50.10.16

❏ **M. et Mme Jospin**
47, rue des Antilles
Cap-Haïtien, Haïti
(509) 17.05.60

❏ **M. et Mme Cœur**
2, place du 6-juin
Lille, France
(33) 20.20.50.40

❏ **M. et Mme Khoury**
30, avenue Anne-de-Bretagne
Tours, France
(33) 47.40.50.20

❏ **M. et Mme Dikembe**
6, rue Mohammed Ben Bella
Alger, Algérie
(213) 022.0451

❏ **M. et Mme Perrochon**
15, avenue de la Flandre
Bruxelles, Belgique
(32) 2.18.20.40

❏ **M. et Mme Thibodeau**
20, avenue de Champlain
Montréal, Québec, Canada
(514) 584-8391

❏ **M. et Mme Poisson**
16, rue Victor-Hugo
Berne, Suisse
(41) 31.20.16.95

Note When you telephone outside of the United States, U.S. territories, or Canada, you need to know the country code and city code. These codes may have one, two, or three digits. In the numbers on the facing page, the country code is in parentheses and the city code is the first part of the rest of the number. If you are calling another country, you need to dial the country code and then the city code before the home number of the person you are calling. If you make a call within the same city, you don't have to dial the country code or the city code. By the way, this rule does not work for Canadian numbers. They work like American ones.

1. What is the **nom de famille** of the homestay family you have chosen? _____

2. What is their country (or area) code? _____

3. What is their city code? _____

4. When you are in your homestay city, what number would you dial to call your homestay

   family if you needed to? _____

C. LA LETTRE ET L'ENVELOPPE

Each student who participates in a homestay writes a letter (**une lettre**) to the host family before the homestay begins. You've chosen your host family and you have their **adresse**. Address an envelope (**une enveloppe**) to them. Put your return address in the upper-left corner. Use the envelope below to practice.

D. LA LETTRE DE JENNIFER

In Element 4, you completed a **Fiche de renseignements personnels** to give your host family some information about yourself. A letter (**une lettre**) is an additional and more personal part of your introduction. Below is the letter Jennifer Johnson wrote to the Laroches last year. Read it three times. Read first for general meaning. (You don't have to know every word to understand the main idea.) Remember to look for cognates. The second time you read the letter, if you need more help, refer to the English meanings of the new words (**mots nouveaux**) written in the side column. Finally, read **la lettre** again for further detail and practice.

le 10 avril

chers Monsieur et Madame Laroche,

Je m'appelle Jennifer Johnson. Je suis élève à Loveland Middle School. J'ai 12 ans. J'aime nager, faire du ski et jouer au football. J'étudie le français.

Voilà une photo de ma famille. Il y a six personnes dans ma famille: mon père, ma mère, mon frère, mes deux sœurs et moi. J'ai aussi un oiseau et un chat.

J'arrive à l'aéroport le 22 juin à une heure de l'après-midi. Le numéro du vol est Air Alpha 622. J'attends ma visite chez vous avec impatience. Merci mille fois.

Mes sentiments les meilleurs,

Jennifer

MOTS NOUVEAUX

Je suis I am
élève student
nager to swim
faire du ski to ski
jouer au football to play soccer
J'étudie I study

Voilà Here is/Here are
une photo a photo
Il y a There is/There are
dans in
frère brother
sœurs sisters
et and
aussi also

J'arrive I arrive
à l'aéroport at the airport
de l'après-midi in the afternoon
du vol of the flight
J'attends I'm waiting for
chez vous at your home

E. TA LETTRE

You've read Jennifer's letter from last year. Below is an outline to help you write your own letter. Use it to complete your first draft. Then, with a partner, read your draft and discuss possible changes. Rewrite a final copy of your letter. You may write this final copy on a nice sheet of stationery or compose it on a computer.

le _____ _____
    (day)   *(month)*

Chers Monsieur et Madame _____ ,

_____ . _____
             (My name is . . .)   *(I am)*

élève à _____ . J'ai _____ ans. _____
       (your school name)   *(your age)*   *(I like)*

_____ et _____ . J'étudie _____ .
   (your favorite activity)   *(your favorite sport)*   *(French)*

Voilà une _____ de ma _____ . _____ _____
        (photo)   *(family)*   *(There are)*   *(total number)*

personnes dans ma famille: _____ .
                           (list of members of your family)

Il y a aussi _____ et _____ . J'arrive
           (list of your pets—number and type)

à l'_____ le _____ à huit heures du soir *(in the evening)*.
      (airport)   *(June 22)*

Le numéro du vol est Beta Air 783. _____ ma visite chez vous avec impatience.
                       (I'm waiting for)

Mes sentiments les meilleurs,

_____
         (your signature)

F. LA RÉPONSE

This is truly exciting! Your host family received your letter and their son, Antoine, answered it. Read the response (**la réponse**) carefully three times. Read first for general meaning. Remember to look for cognates. The second time, if you need more help, refer to the English meanings of the **mots nouveaux** written in the side column. Then, read it again for further detail and practice.

le 15 avril

Salut!

Je m'appelle Antoine. Merci pour ta lettre et les photos. Elles sont bien. Je suis élève en cours moyen 2. Mon école s'appelle l'académie centrale. J'ai 12 ans. J'aime nager, jouer au football et jouer au tennis. J'étudie l'anglais. Nous avons beaucoup en commun.

Voilà une photo de ma famille. Il y a quatre personnes dans ma famille. Ma sœur s'appelle Valérie. Je n'ai pas de frère. J'ai deux amis. Ils s'appellent Frédéric et Jérôme. J'aime les animaux domestiques. J'ai un chien et un oiseau, mais je n'ai pas de chat.

J'attends ta visite. Il y a beaucoup à faire ici. N'oublie pas ta raquette de tennis. Il y a un court de tennis près de chez moi. Tu as déjà mon adresse et mon numéro de téléphone.

À bientôt,
Antoine

MOTS NOUVEAUX

Salut! Hi!
Elles sont bien. They're great.
en cours moyen 2 in the 7th grade
aussi too
jouer au tennis to play tennis
J'étudie l'anglais I study English
Ma sœur s'appelle My sister's name is
Ils s'appellent Their names are
J'attends I'm waiting for
ta visite your visit
beaucoup à faire a lot to do
N'oublie pas Don't forget
ta raquette de tennis your tennis raquet
un court de tennis tennis court
près de chez moi near my house
Tu as déjà You already have
À bientôt See you soon

G. PHOTOS DE LA FAMILLE

Pictures, as well as letters, help you get better acquainted with your homestay family. After reading Antoine's **lettre**, locate the pictures of the family (**photos de la famille**), friends, and pets on page 50. Then look at their pictures below. Write their names below the pictures. This will help you recognize Antoine's family and friends when you arrive.

La famille d'Antoine

Les amis d'Antoine

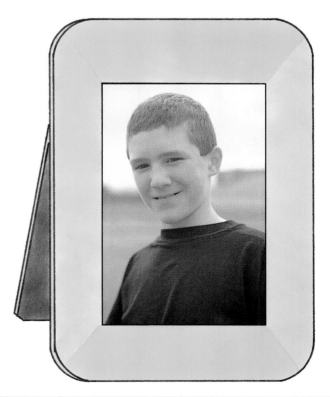

H. LA PREMIÈRE IMPRESSIONÈ

Have you heard the saying, "One picture is worth a thousand words?" Do you think it's true? Pictures often give us our first impression (**la première impression**) of people. Look at **les photos de la famille d'Antoine**. What are your first impressions? Now look below at some French words that can be used to describe someone's personality. Choose one of these words to describe each important person in Antoine's life. Write that word by the appropriate picture on page 57. Be careful! There's also another saying that "looks can be deceiving." After meeting them, you may change your **première impression**. Some of the words have two forms. If you need help selecting the correct form of a word, go back to Element 2 or ask your teacher.

extroverti(e)	égoïste	courageux(-euse)	généreux(-euse)
timide	travailleur(-euse)	obéissant(e)	jaloux(-ouse)
sentimental(e)	affectueux(-euse)	ambitieux(-euse)	bavard(e)
indépendant(e)	arrogant(e)	spontané(e)	aimable
paresseux(-euse)	actif(-ive)	indécis(e)	calme

I. DES IMPRESSIONS

You've learned some French words to describe personality characteristics and given your first impressions of Antoine's family. Now, think about yourself. Look at the list of characteristics in Activity H. Choose your two strongest positive characteristics and write them in the blank in the sentence beginning with **Je suis** *(I am)*.

Je suis _____ et _____ .

Next, think of someone you know and admire. Write his or her name in the first blank of the following sentence. Complete the sentence by listing five characteristics you see in the person you chose.

_____ est *(is)* _____ , _____ ,

_____ , _____ et _____ .

Share the description above with a partner. Talk more about why you admire the person you chose to describe.

Teenagers in France

J. UN CADEAU

When a French-speaking person stays in someone's home, he or she brings a gift (**un cadeau**). When you participate in a homestay experience, it is important to do things that are culturally appropriate and show your good manners. **Un cadeau** is your way of saying thank you to your host family for opening their home to you and letting you participate in their lives. This **cadeau** is also a way of sharing a part of your culture. It does not have to be big and expensive, but it should be selected with thoughtfulness and care. Your host family might particularly enjoy something you have made or a special souvenir of the city, state, or region where you live, such as local handicrafts or products or a book of pictures about your area.

For help in choosing a gift, look at the idea webs below. Working with two or three of your classmates, brainstorm ideas for these webs. Fill in the cells with suggestions from your group. If you wish, add additional cells. Then, when you have all shared your ideas, try to agree on the most appropriate gift.

CADEAUX

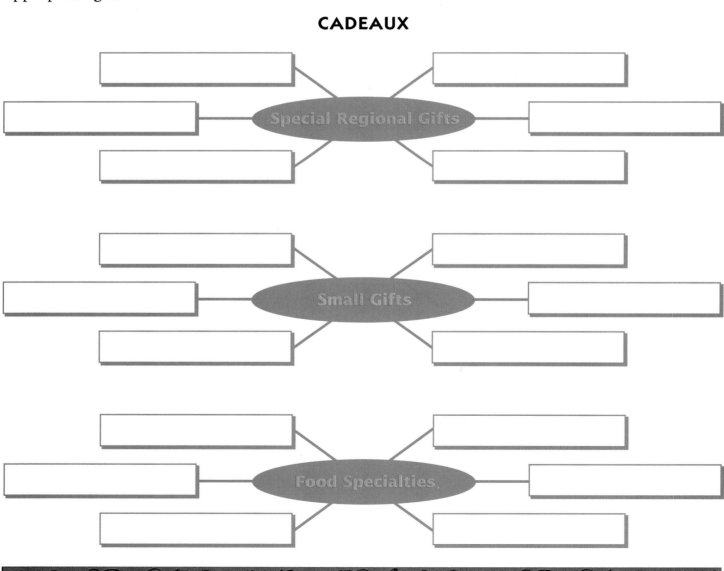

K. MON JOURNAL

Select five to ten new French words from this Element that you need to remember. Write them under **Mes mots.** Under **Cadeau** include a drawing or a picture of the gift you have chosen to give your host family. Also, record new information in your journal under **Nouveaux renseignements**. You may want to include the **lettre** you wrote to your host family or you may want to describe your first impression of someone you met recently.

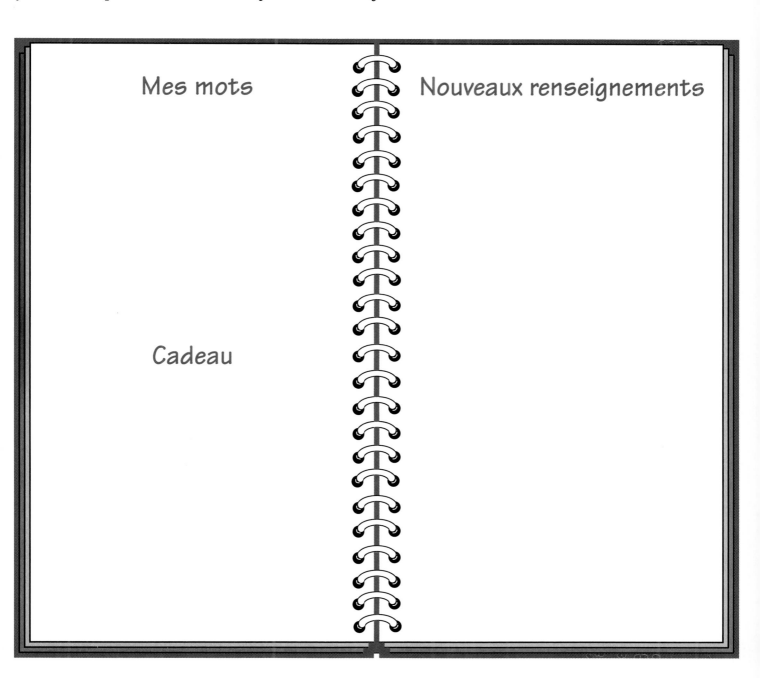

Mes mots

Cadeau

Nouveaux renseignements

PREPARING A PHOTO ALBUM

PERSPECTIVE

In Elements 1 through 5, you have prepared for your homestay experience. You've learned about your homestay country, chosen a host family, packed your clothes, applied for a **passeport**, written to your host family, and received a letter from them. You're almost ready to go! In Element 6, you are going to construct a photo album that organizes **photos** and special memories (**les souvenirs**) about your life in the United States to show to your host family and new friends.

Your album is also a review of the French you have learned in Elements 1 through 5. Your teacher may give you an Organization and Assessment Grid to help assess your project. As you organize your album (**ton album**), keep the criteria on the grid in mind. Have fun! **Amusez-vous bien!**

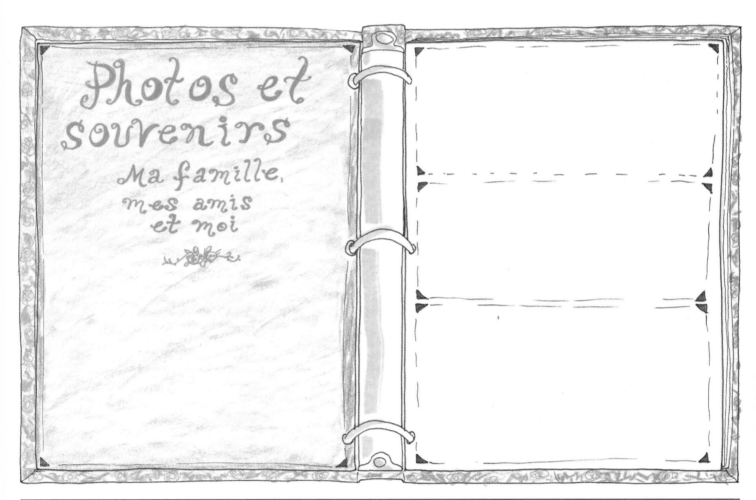

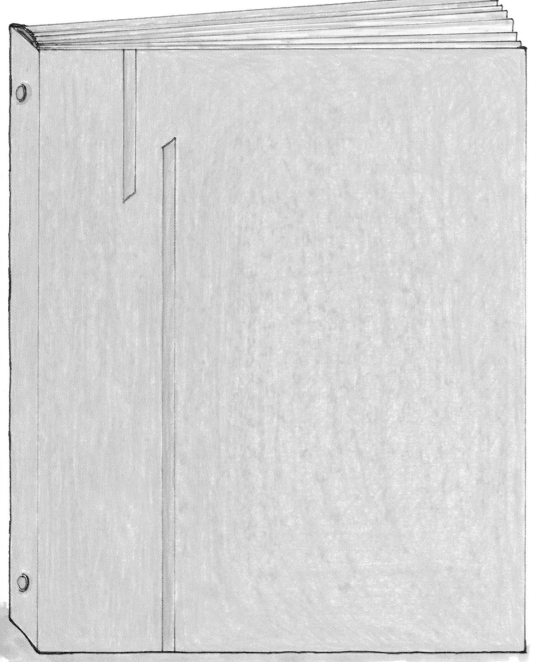

A. TA VIE

Your homestay family will want to see what your life (**ta vie**) is like in the United States. To show them, you will construct a photo album to take with you on your homestay. It is a reflection of you, your family, your friends, your neighborhood, and your favorite activities and sports. Remember that your host family speaks French, so you'll need to use as much French as possible in your album. Begin by designing a cover page for your album. As you prepare your album, think about what is important in your daily life.

B. MOI

Your host family will want to get to know you when you arrive. Your photo album is an interesting way to share your life with them. Start the album by showing yourself and all the things you like to do. **Moi** means *me*. Place a photo or a drawing (**un dessin**) of yourself in each square labeled **Moi.** Write some information about yourself below each picture. To get you started, some suggested sentences are started below. Don't limit yourself to the starter sentences, however. Be creative. There may be many things you'd like to share with your host family through **photos** or **dessins**. Be sure to label each photo or drawing in French. If you need help, use a dictionary or ask your classmates or teacher.

MOI

Je m'appelle _____ .

Mon anniversaire est le _____ .

J'ai _____ ans.

_____

_____

MOI

J'aime _____

_____ .

Je suis _____

_____ .

C. MA FAMILLE

Your host family and new friends will also be very interested in your family (**ta famille**). Place photos or drawings of your family in the squares labeled **Ma famille.** Write some information about them below the picture. Use the sentence starters if you want, but don't limit yourself to them. You may want to include additional information about your family. Maybe you can tell what they are like. If you need help, use a dictionary or ask your classmates or teacher.

MA FAMILLE

Dans ma famille, il y a _____ personnes.

Mon père s'appelle _____ .

Il a _____ ans. *(He is ___ years old.)*

Ma mère s'appelle _____ .

Elle a _____ ans. *(She is ___ years old.)*

MA FAMILLE

Mes frères et mes sœurs s'appellent

_____ .

Ils ont _____ ans.

(They are ___ years old.)

D. MA MAISON ET MON QUARTIER

Your home (**ta maison**) and your neighborhood (**ton quartier**) will be interesting to your home-stay family. They'll want to know how they differ from **maisons** or **appartements** and **quartiers** in their country. Show pictures of your home and neighborhood so that your homestay family will have a clear idea of what they are like. Describe your home and neighborhood from the pictures.

MA MAISON

Mon adresse est_____

_____

_____

Mon numéro de téléphone est le _____

_____ .

MON QUARTIER

Mon quartier s'appelle_____.

Il se trouve à _____
                        (city, state)

_____ .

Dans mon quartier il y a_____
                              (points of interest)

_____

_____ .

E. MES AMIS/AMIES

You'll make new friends while you're on your homestay. They will want to know about your friends (**tes amis**) in your hometown. Include **photos** or **dessins** and descriptions of your friends in your album. Use the words you learned earlier to describe their characteristics and personalities. Place the pictures in the spaces labeled **Mes amis/amies**.

MES AMIS/AMIES

Mes amis/amies s'appellent _____

_____

_____ .

Ils/Elles ont _____ ans.

MES AMIS/AMIES

Ils/Elles aiment (*They like*) _____

_____ .

Ils/Elles sont_____
(*description*)

_____

_____

_____ .

F. MON ÉCOLE

You'll attend school in your homestay country, too. While you're there, the new teachers and students will be curious about the school you attend in your hometown. Include a **photo** or **dessin** of your school in the space labeled **Mon école.** Also put a picture of your class in the space labeled **Ma classe.** Then write information about your school and class that your new friends will find interesting.

MON ÉCOLE

Mon école s'appelle _____ .

Il y a _____ élèves dans mon école.

Mon école se trouve à _____
                                    (city)
_____ .

MA CLASSE

Mon professeur s'appelle _____

_____ .

Il y a _____ élèves dans ma classe.

G. MES ACTIVITÉS PRÉFÉRÉES

Every student has favorite activities. In your **Fiche de renseignements personnels** and your **lettre**, you talked about your **activités préférées**. In your album, put photos and drawings that show how you spend your free time. Show at least one on each page of your album. Don't show sports. You'll do that on the next page of your album.

MES ACTIVITÉS PRÉFÉRÉES

J'aime _____

_____

_____

_____ .

AUTRES ACTIVITÉS PRÉFÉRÉES

J'aime aussi _____

_____

_____

_____ .

H. MES SPORTS PRÉFÉRÉS

You may also want to tell your host family about your favorite sports: those you play and those you watch. In your album, put photos and drawings that show you playing your **sports préférés** or that show the kinds of **sports** you like to watch. Show at least one on each page of your album.

MES SPORTS PRÉFÉRÉS

J'aime _____

_____

_____

_____ .

AUTRES SPORTS PRÉFÉRÉS

J'aime aussi _____

_____

_____

_____ .

I. MON ANIMAL DOMESTIQUE ET AUTRES CHOSES IMPORTANTES

Pets (**les animaux domestiques**) are an important part of many students' lives. If you have **un animal domestique**, remember to include a picture of it in your album. If you don't have a pet, show the kind of pet you might like to have. Then write some information about the pet below the picture.

Everyone has other important things (**d'autres choses importantes**) in his or her daily life that make him or her unique. Think about some other important things that you would like to share with your homestay family and friends. Include drawings or photos if you want to, and write information about these things.

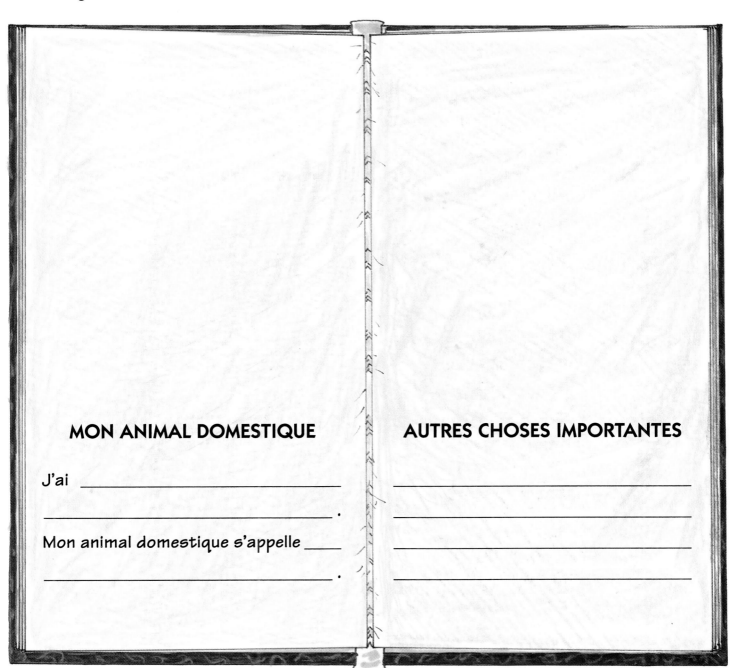

MON ANIMAL DOMESTIQUE

J'ai _____

_____.

Mon animal *domestique s'appelle* ____

_____.

AUTRES CHOSES IMPORTANTES

_____

_____

_____

7 ARRIVAL

PERSPECTIVE

After weeks of preparation, your actual homestay adventure begins. This Element prepares you to arrive in your homestay country and meet your host family. You learn to greet people and make introductions in French. In addition, you become an international traveler who understands arrival times, international time-zone changes, and airport procedures. **Prêt(e)? Allons-y!**

VILLE	VOL		HEURE
LOS ANGELES	BETA	901	2:00
BOSTON	DELTA	283	5:00
NEW YORK	AMERICAN	606	9:00
DENVER	ALPHA	622	13:00
PORT AU PRINCE	PAN AM	742	13:00
DETROIT	BETA	527	17:00
TORONTO	AIR CANADA	831	19:00

A. L'ITINÉRAIRE

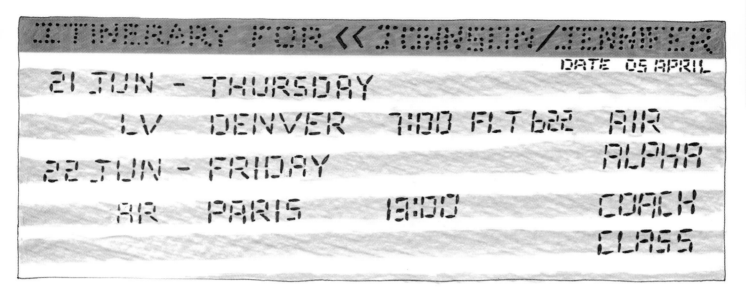

Last year, the itinerary (**l'itinéraire**) Jennifer received from her travel agent looked like the one above. At first, she was not sure how to read the arrival time because the information was written using the 24-hour clock. When you receive your travel itinerary, you'll need to know how to interpret 24-hour time. You want to be sure to be on time for your flight, and you'll need to let your host family know exactly when you are arriving. The 24-hour clock is frequently used by airlines to indicate arrival and departure times. It's not hard to understand 24-hour time when you know the system.

Using the 24-hour clock avoids possible confusion between A.M. and P.M. In Europe and many other parts of the world, it is used in schedules and timetables. When speaking, however, people normally use the 12-hour way of expressing time.

In the 24-hour system, the hours for 1:00 A.M. to 12:00 P.M. are the same as they are in the 12-hour system. For hours later than 12:00 P.M., subtract 12 hours from the time to find out the corresponding P.M. time. For example, here's how to figure out what time 14:00 would be:

14:00 –12 hours = 2:00 P.M.

Midnight (12 A.M.)is written as **0:00.**

Ready for some practice? Let's try! **Essayons!**

13:00 _____   20:00 _____

16:00 _____   21:00 _____

19:00 _____   0:00 _____

B. RENSEIGNEMENTS SUR LE VOL

Read the **renseignements sur le vol** *(flight information)* for the trip to your homestay country. Pay careful attention to the flight number and to the departure and arrival times.

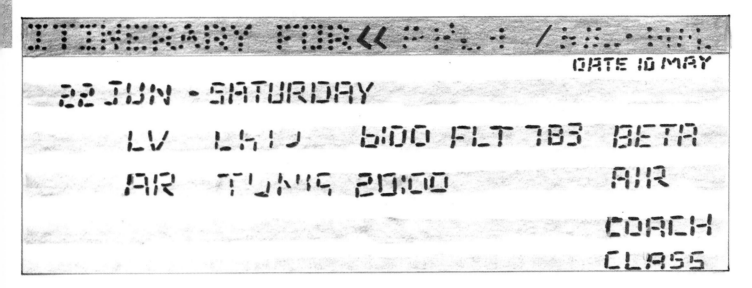

You need to remind your host family about when to meet you at the airport (**à l'aéroport**). A postcard (**une carte postale**) is a quick way to tell when your flight (**ton vol**) is arriving. Complete the following **carte postale** with the information from your travel itinerary. Use the **adresse** for your host family that you learned in Element 5.

C. TA MONTRE

In Element 4, when you learned about telling time, your teacher may have talked about time zones. When you travel from coast to coast in the United States or overseas, you pass through different time zones. Now that you're ready for your trip, you need to understand how time-zone changes work. Remember to change your watch (**ta montre**) to show the local time in your home-stay country. You can make this change during your flight or when you arrive at your destination.

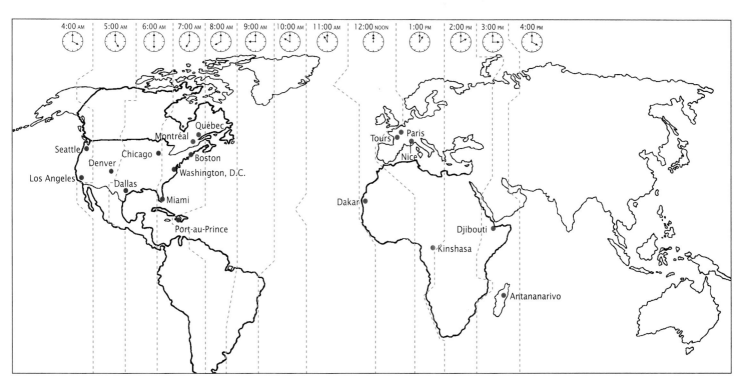

Using the time-zone map above, calculate the time changes that occur when you travel between the cities listed below. Each time in the middle column shows what time it is in the city you flew from. In the third column, write the correct local time.

From _____ to _____	When you arrive, your watch says	You need to change your watch to say
1. Boston to Antananarivo	5:00 A.M.	_____
2. Los Angeles to Québec	8:00 A.M.	_____
3. Denver to Nice	11:00 A.M.	_____
4. Dallas to Djibouti	1:00 A.M.	_____
5. Chicago to Kinshasa	4:00 A.M.	_____
6. Miami to Paris	7:00 A.M.	_____

D. LA DOUANE

When you arrive at the airport in your homestay country, your plane will land at the international terminal. First, you must pass through the customs and immigration (**la douane**) where your passport is checked and stamped.

As you pass through **la douane**, you are greeted in French. You are also asked some simple questions about where you come from and how long you plan to stay in your homestay country. To get ready, read the following conversation quietly to yourself. Your teacher will help you with the meaning of the new words and phrases.

Le douanier:	**Bonjour.**
Toi:	**Bonjour.**
Le douanier:	**D'où viens-tu?**
Toi:	**Des États-Unis.**
Le douanier:	**Tu vas rester combien de temps?**
Toi:	**Vingt et un jours.**
Le douanier:	**Très bien. Merci.**

Now follow these steps:

1. Listen as your teacher presents the conversation.

2. Then listen again and repeat the words and phrases.

3. Next, your teacher will read the role of **le douanier** (*customs officer*). Answer by reading your role.

4. Finally, working with a partner, practice the conversation several times. Take turns being the official.

Are you ready to go through **la douane**? **Allons-y!**

E. BIENVENUE!

After going through **la douane**, you will meet your host family in the arrival area. To prepare for this meeting, listen to the following conversation between Jennifer and the Laroches. Making a recording of this conversation was one way Jennifer kept some memories of her visit. Listen carefully! You can use the same greetings when you meet your host family.

MOTS NOUVEAUX

Bienvenue. Welcome.
Merci. Thank you.
Ça va? How are you?
Ça va. Fine.
Je vous remercie. Thank you.
Je suis enchanté(e) de faire votre connaissance. I'm glad to meet you.

Je suis... I am . . .
Le voyage s'est bien passé? Did the trip go well?
très bien very well
mais but
je suis un peu fatigué(e) I'm a little tired.
Salut! Hi!

F. SALUTATIONS

In the conversation in Activity E, you learned several greetings (**salutations**) and new expressions in French. These expressions are useful when meeting people in French-speaking countries. Working with a partner, practice each of the four short dialogues, changing roles each time.

Now, form groups of five students and practice the entire conversation (all four dialogues). Each of you should take one of the roles: father, mother, Claude, François, and Jennifer. Practice introducing yourselves to each other. Change roles after each complete conversation.

G. EXERÇONS-NOUS!

Let's practice! (**Exerçons-nous!**) To remember the French expressions used for meeting and greeting, complete the following activity. Write the letter of each French expression in the blank next to its English meaning.

1. _____ Nice to meet you.   **a. Bienvenue.**

2. _____ Did the trip go well?   **b. Je m'appelle...**

3. _____ How are you?   **c. Je suis enchanté(e) de faire votre connaissance.**

4. _____ Welcome.   **d. Je suis un peu fatigué(e).**

5. _____ My name is . . .   **e. Je suis...**

6. _____ I'm a little tired.   **f. Ça va?**

7. _____ I am (I'm) . . .   **g. Le voyage s'est bien passé?**

H. MA VALISE N'EST PAS LÀ!

After meeting your host family, you go to the baggage claim area. All baggage is placed in this area when it comes off the plane. Inside your airline ticket folder, you'll find your baggage claim ticket with the number of your suitcase (**le numéro de ta valise**).

Sometimes it happens. A piece of luggage ends up on the wrong airplane. Now you know why it's important to pack a few necessities in a small piece of carry-on luggage like your **sac à dos.** The airline will find your luggage. To help them, you need to fill out the following baggage claim form. Remember to use the **adresse** and **numéro de téléphone** of your host family. Look back at Element 5 if you need to check their name, address, and phone number.

Réclamation de bagages perdus

Nom de famille _____   Prénom _____

Adresse _____

Ville _____

Téléphone _____

Ligne aérienne _____   Numéro du vol _____

Description de la valise:

❑ grande   ❑ petite

❑ bleue   ❑ noire   ❑ rouge   ❑ marron   ❑ verte

❑ autre couleur _____

I. UN COUP DE TÉLÉPHONE AUX ÉTATS-UNIS

Your baggage claim form is filed. The airline will deliver the suitcase to you as soon as it is found. It's time for you and your host family to leave the airport and drive to their home. Before leaving the airport, you want to make a phone call to the United States (**un coup de téléphone aux États-Unis**) to let your own family know that you have arrived safely. Remember that the times will be different between your homestay country and your hometown in the United States. Is this a good time to make a call? Let's practice with time zones before you decide. Look at the time-zone map on page 75 and complete the following chart. The first one is done for you.

Homestay City, Country	Time	U.S.A. City, State	U.S.A. Time
1. Tours, France	4:00 P.M.	Washington, D.C.	10:00 A.M.
2. Montréal, Québec	7:00 P.M.	Denver, Colorado	——————
3. Dakar, Sénégal	3:00 P.M.	Seattle, Washington	——————
4. Port-au-Prince, Haïti	9:00 A.M.	Dallas, Texas	——————

Now complete the chart with your own personal information:

My Homestay Country	Time	My U.S.A. City, State	Time at home
——————————	3:00 P.M.	——————————	——————

Is this a good time to call? ——————————

J. MON JOURNAL

The baggage-claim manager has called to say that your suitcase has been found. The airline is going to deliver it later today. Remember to tip the delivery person when the luggage arrives. What a busy day! Think of all you have learned about traveling. Write this information under **Nouveaux renseignements**. Select five to ten new French words and phrases from this Element. Write them under **Mes mots.** Put a drawing of something you want to remember about your travels under **Mon dessin**.

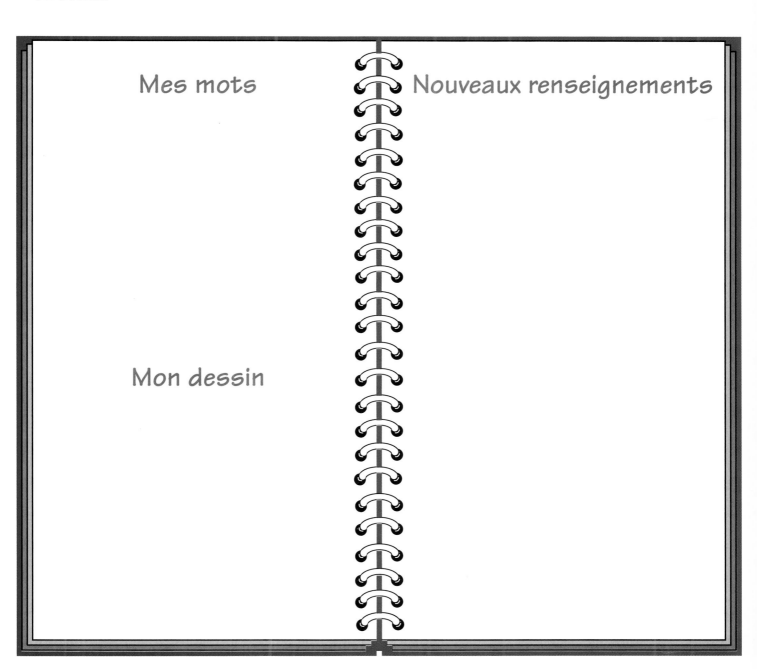

Mes mots

Nouveaux renseignements

Mon dessin

8 YOUR HOMESTAY HOUSE AND DAILY ROUTINE

PERSPECTIVE

When you arrive at your host family's house, you need to find your way around and get settled. You've had a long trip. You look forward to a snack, a rest, and getting to know the daily routine with your host family. Your homestay has begun.

A. J'AI FAIM

After your trip from the airport, your host mother asks if you'd like a snack. You answer politely, **Oui, merci. J'ai faim!** (*Yes, thank you. I'm hungry!*) She invites you into the kitchen to show you where you can find something to eat. To teach you how to make a typical local snack, she prepares a **tartine au chocolat** for you. Here's this easy recipe in French. The first part of the recipe lists the ingredients. Do you understand the meanings of the French words? The pictures will help you understand their meanings.

| **le pain** | **une tranche de pain** | **le chocolat** | **le beurre** | **une tartine au chocolat** |

Now you know the ingredients of **une tartine au chocolat**. Here are the directions for making a piece. Read the directions twice. First read to get a general idea of what you are supposed to do. Try to guess the meaning of any new words. Then read the directions again. This time, if you need more help, refer to the English meanings under **Mots nouveaux** in the side column.

1. **Coupe** une tranche de pain.
2. **Casse** le chocolat en petits **morceaux**.
3. **Mets un peu de** beurre **sur** la tranche de pain.
4. Mets le chocolat sur la tranche de pain **beurrée**.
5. **Mange** la **tartine**.

Bon appétit!

MOTS NOUVEAUX
Coupe Cut
Casse Break
morceaux pieces
Mets Put
un peu de a little
sur on
beurrée buttered
Mange Eat
tartine open-face sandwich

Note — French speakers often say "**Bon appétit!**" before beginning a meal or a snack. It's their way of saying, *"Enjoy the food!"*

Practice making **une tartine au chocolat** at home. Then work with a group of your classmates. Decide how much of each ingredient you'll need to prepare a **tartine au chocolat** for your classmates. Then make some **tartines au chocolat** for them!

Do you know of any other foods that are common in your homestay country? What are they? If you don't know, where can you go to find out? Ask your teacher or the media center specialist to help you find this information. Then prepare a report for your class. Your report may be written or oral, or you may present visuals or a demonstration.

B. LES PIÈCES DE LA MAISON

After your snack, you are ready to learn about the house (**la maison**) where you'll be living. Look at the picture below. It shows the rooms of the house (**les pièces de la maison**). Listen as your teacher names them in French. Do any of the names sound similar to English?

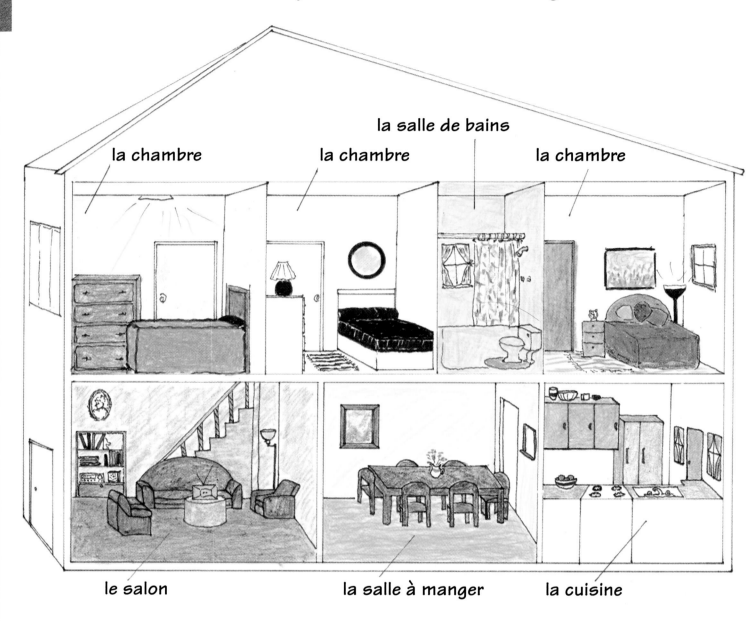

la salle de bains

la chambre la chambre la chambre

le salon la salle à manger la cuisine

Let's take a tour **de la maison**. Your teacher will say the name of a room in French. Repeat that name after your teacher as you point to the room in the picture.

C. L'INSTALLATION

You've had a tour of your new **maison**. Now it's time to learn the French words for furniture and other household items (**l'installation**). Below are pictures of these items. Listen while your teacher names each item in French. Notice that the name of each item has **le** or **la** in front of it. Both are French words for *the*. You learned about **le** and **la** with items of clothing and travel in Element 2. **L'évier** has **L'**, which is the form **le** and **la** take before a vowel.

la baignoire   le lit   la cuisinière   la douche   le bureau   la radio

le lavabo   l'évier   la lampe   la lampe   la table   la table   le frigo

la chaise   le fauteuil   le canapé   la télé   la serviette

Exerçons-nous! Look at the pictures again. Cover the labels. Working with a partner, take turns practicing the names of the items in French. Partner A points to the picture of an item. Partner B identifies the item in French. Reverse roles each time an item is named. Then take turns pointing to all of the items, one at a time, until your partner gets one wrong. Then switch roles. Which partner is the first one to name them all correctly?

D. FINIS L'INSTALLATION!

To do this activity, you'll need pictures of furniture and other household items. You can cut these out from old magazines, catalogues, or the hand-out your teacher gives you. You may also draw your own. On the opposite page is the floor plan of **la maison**. Put the furniture and other household items in the rooms. (**Finis l'installation.**)

Follow these steps:

1. Cut out or draw pictures of furniture and other household items.
2. Place the pictures on your desk so that you can see all of them.
3. Listen as your teacher says the name of an item.
4. Place the picture of the item in the appropriate room as you repeat the name quietly to yourself.
5. Check your progress with your teacher.

Partner practice: Take turns with a partner describing the location of the item.

1. Partner A tells Partner B to put an item in a specific location. For example: **Mets la radio dans la chambre.**
2. Partner B repeats the name of the item and places its picture in the appropriate room.
3. Partner A verifies the item and its location by saying **Oui** or **Non**.
4. When all of the items are positioned, change roles.

When you're sure you know the French names for all the furniture and other household items **de** (*of*) **la maison**, paste the pictures on the floor plan. Label each picture on the floor plan in French.

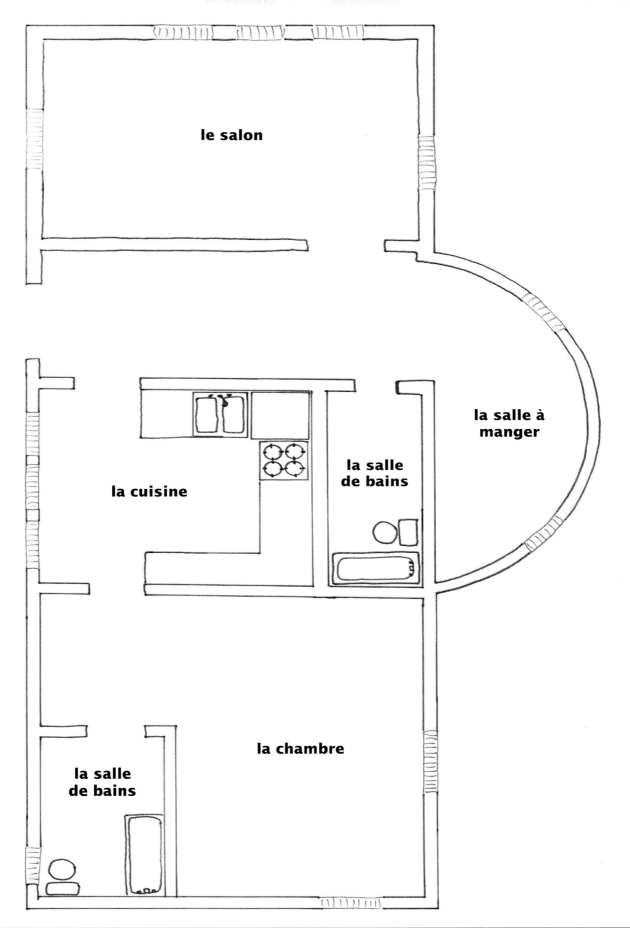

le salon

la salle à
manger

la cuisine

la salle
de bains

la chambre

la salle
de bains

E. UNE JOURNÉE AVEC ANTOINE

You've learned your way around **la maison** and you're beginning to feel at home. To feel more like a member of the family, during your homestay, you want to follow the family routine. To do this, you need to understand and use some key phrases. Look at the pictures below. They show Antoine doing some of the activities of his day (**journée**). Listen as your teacher tells in French what he is doing. Next, point to each picture and repeat the French sentence after your teacher.

1. Antoine se lève.

2. Antoine prend le petit déjeuner.

3. Antoine va à l'école.

4. Antoine déjeune.

5. Antoine joue avec ses copains.

6. Antoine fait ses devoirs.

7. Antoine regarde la télé.

8. Antoine dîne.

9. Antoine se couche.

Note Notice that item 5 above uses a new word for friends. **Copain** (a male friend) and **copine** (a female friend) are used for those who are not your closest friends. Your closest friends are called your **amis/amies**.

Now, write the letter of each picture by the sentence that describes it.

_____ 1. Antoine dîne.   a.

_____ 2. Antoine fait ses devoirs.   b.

_____ 3. Antoine déjeune.   c.

_____ 4. Antoine regarde la télé.   d.

_____ 5. Antoine joue avec ses copains.   e.

_____ 6. Antoine se lève.   f.

_____ 7. Antoine prend le petit déjeuner.   g.

_____ 8. Antoine va à l'école.   h.

_____ 9. Antoine se couche.   i.

F. QUAND?

You've learned the French phrases to describe Antoine's activities in **une journée avec Antoine**. But when (**quand?**) does he do each activity? You already know how to say on-the-hour times in French. Here are the words you need to say other times:

et quart	*quarter after, quarter past,* or *15 minutes past the hour*
et demie	*half past* or *30 minutes past the hour*
moins	*before the hour*
moins le quart	*quarter to* or 15 *minutes before the hour*

Here are some examples.

When?	Time	Answer
Quand?	3 h 05	**à trois heures cinq**
Quand?	3 h 15	**à trois heures et quart**
Quand?	3 h 30	**à trois heures et demie**
Quand?	3 h 45	**à quatre heures moins le quart**
Quand?	3 h 55	**à quatre heures moins cinq**

Now, fill in the blanks to tell the time shown on each clock.

Quand?

1. à _____ heures

2. à neuf heures _____ _____

3. à neuf heures _____ _____ _____

4. à neuf heures _____

5. à neuf heures _____ _____

6. à neuf heures _____ _____

G. L'EMPLOI DU TEMPS D'ANTOINE

While you are eating dinner, your host family talks about Antoine's schedule (**l'emploi du temps d'Antoine**). After dinner, you go over his **emploi du temps** with your host mother. She gives you the specific times in **l'emploi du temps d'Antoine.** Listen to the **emploi du temps** and write the times of day (using numerals) in your notebook. (Your teacher may play the role of your host mother.)

Example: You hear: **Antoine se lève à six heures et quart.**
                   You see: **Antoine se lève à _____ .**
                   You write: **6 h 15**

Work with a partner. Read Antoine's activities and the times you wrote in French. Compare the schedules you each wrote. Check your responses with your teacher.

1. Antoine prend le petit déjeuner à _____.

2. Antoine va à l'école à _____.

3. Antoine déjeune à _____.

4. Antoine fait ses devoirs à _____.

5. Antoine joue avec ses copains à _____.

6. Antoine dîne à _____.

7. Antoine regarde la télé à _____.

8. Antoine se couche à _____.

H. TON EMPLOI DU TEMPS

Your schedule (**ton emploi du temps**) with your homestay family is very similar to that of Antoine. Look at the pictures below. These are the same activities Antoine's mother talked about in Activity G. Now, Antoine wants to compare his schedule with yours in the United States. You need to know how to say *I* when telling him about your schedule. *I* in French is **Je**. Listen as your teacher uses **Je** when describing each of the activities in the pictures. Listen again and point to each picture, repeating the phrase you use when telling Antoine about **ton emploi du temps**.

1. Je me lève.

2. Je prends le petit déjeuner.

3. Je vais à l'école.

4. Je déjeune.

5. Je joue avec mes copains/ mes copines.

6. Je fais mes devoirs.

7. Je regarde la télé.

8. Je dîne.

9. Je me couche.

Using the pictures and sentences on the opposite page, complete the **emploi du temps** below by telling the times of day you usually do the activities. Remember to begin each sentence with **Je** and complete the sentence with a time of day. The first one is done for you.

1. _Je me lève à_
   _6 h 15._
   _____

2. _____
   _____
   _____

3. _____
   _____
   _____

4. _____
   _____
   _____

5. _____
   _____
   _____

6. _____
   _____
   _____

7. _____
   _____
   _____

8. _____
   _____
   _____

9. _____
   _____
   _____

J. UNE INTERVIEW AVEC TES COPAINS/COPINES

Les emplois du temps (*schedules*) vary from country to country. They also vary from household to household. Conduct an interview with your friends (**une interview avec tes copains/copines**) to find out about their schedules. Then fill in the chart below. First, show the time of day you do each of the three activities. Then show the times given to you by two of your **copains/copines**.

Je me lève à _____.

Copain/Copine A se lève à _____.

Copain/Copine B se lève à _____.

Je déjeune à _____.

Copain/Copine A déjeune à _____.

Copain/Copine B déjeune à _____.

Je me couche à _____.

Copain/Copine A se couche à _____.

Copain/Copine B se couche à _____.

K. MON JOURNAL

You have had an opportunity to learn about the daily routine in your new host family. In **ton journal** write about your routine under **Nouveaux renseignements.** Select five to ten new French words or phrases from this Element. Write them under **Mes mots.** Put a drawing of something you learned during your first day with your host family under **Mon dessin.**

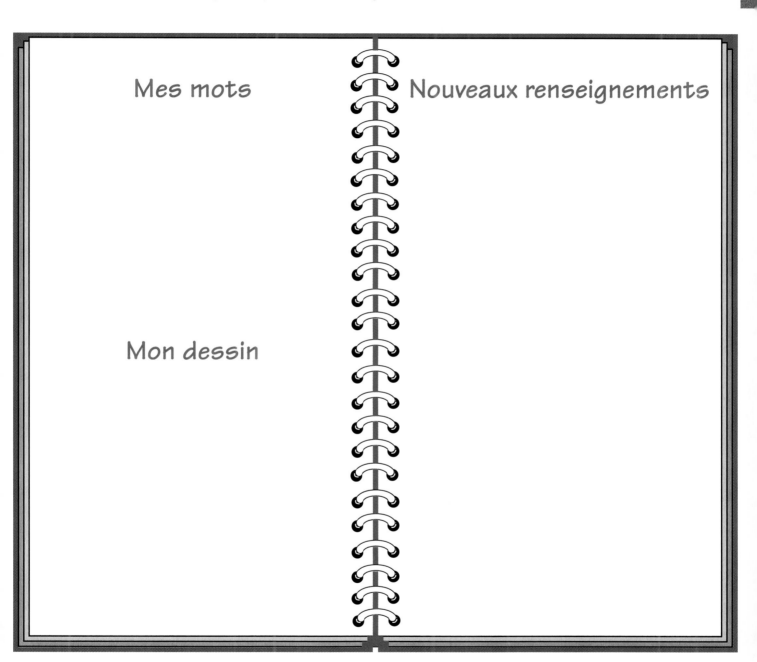

Mes mots

Nouveaux renseignements

Mon dessin

GETTING AROUND TOWN

PERSPECTIVE

Among the most exciting attractions in a city are its local sights and cuisine. In this Element, you learn how to get around in your host city and enjoy a meal in a local restaurant.

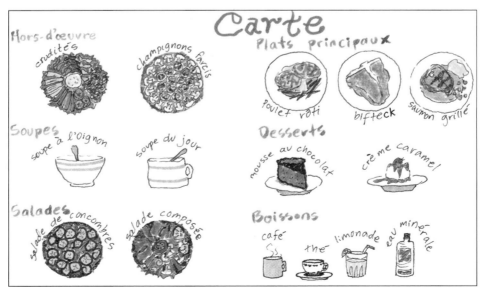

A. LES PANNEAUX ET LES ENSEIGNES EN VILLE

 Enseignes are signs on stores and other buildings. **Panneaux** are other street signs.

You are excited about getting to know your new city (**ville**). Your host family has promised to take you sightseeing. In the meantime, you see signs (**enseignes et panneaux**) everywhere and you want to explore on your own. Look at **les panneaux et les enseignes** below. Now look at the list of things to do. Which sign would you look for to find the place where you do each of the following activities? Match each of the **enseignes et panneaux** to the reason why you would go to that place.

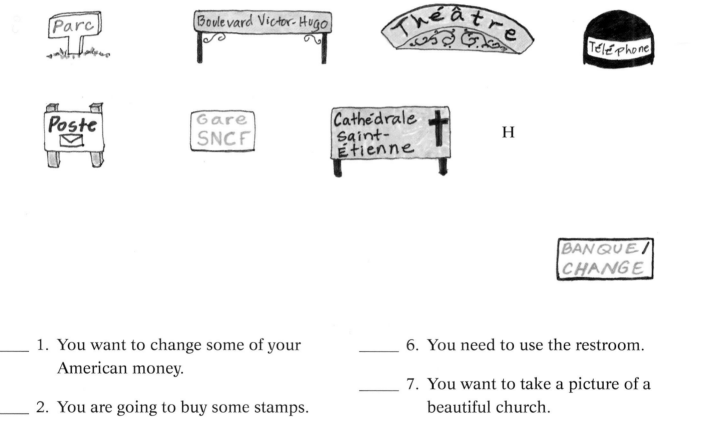

_____ 1. You want to change some of your American money.

_____ 2. You are going to buy some stamps.

_____ 3. You want to see the main street, which is named after a very famous French-speaking historical figure.

_____ 4. You want to see a French play.

_____ 5. You want to see all the beautiful gardens.

_____ 6. You need to use the restroom.

_____ 7. You want to take a picture of a beautiful church.

_____ 8. You want to make a telephone call.

_____ 9. You would like to see a movie.

_____10. You need to get a train schedule.

B. EXPRESSIONS IMPORTANTES

Expressions importantes

1. J'ai faim. _____
2. J'ai soif. _____
3. Je suis malade. _____
4. Je me suis perdu(e). _____
5. Pardon. Pouvez-vous m'aider?. _____
6. Je voudrais un Coca. _____
7. Où est la banque? _____
8. Où sont les toilettes? _____
9. S'il vous plaît. _____
10. Merci. _____

Above are ten important expressions (**expressions importantes**). Look at the pictures your teacher shows you and repeat each phrase. Now with a partner, guess the English meaning of each **expression**. Write your prediction on the line following the phrase. Check them with your teacher.

 Note If you want to say *please* to a friend or to anyone younger than about 18 years old, you should say **s'il te plaît**.

C. DIRECTIONS

In addition to the **expressions importantes** you have learned, there are some other words you need to know to understand and follow directions. Listen and watch carefully while your teacher models some directions and positions in French. Repeat them after your teacher. Then practice demonstrating them with a partner or a small group. Do you think you can follow directions well enough now to find your way around town?

Tourne à droite.

Tourne à gauche.

Va tout droit.

derrière

devant

à côté de

D. LE PLAN DE LA VILLE

Here's a chance to see how well you can follow directions in French. You need to go to the bank (**la banque**) to exchange some American dollars for local currency. Your host mother told you that there is **une banque** near the house. Look at the map (**le plan**) of the neighborhood. Put your finger on the building labeled **Ma maison**. This is where you will start. Move your finger along the streets according to your teacher's directions. Which building is **la banque**? What letter represents **la banque**? Put that letter in this blank: _____.

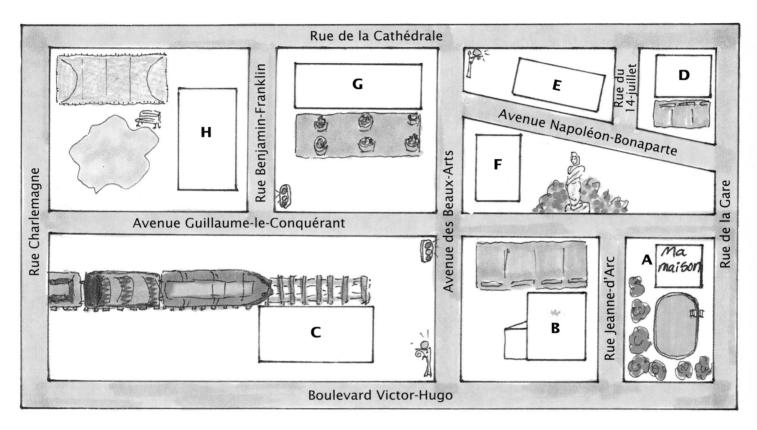

E. EXERÇONS-NOUS!

Look again at **le plan de la ville**. Your teacher will give you directions to four different places. At the beginning of each set of directions, put your pencil on the building labeled **Ma maison**. This is where you will start. Listen to the directions your teacher gives you. Follow the directions with your pencil. Where are you? Write the name of the building or place in the correct box provided on the map above.

F. LA PLACE

In the center of many French-speaking cities is a town square, **la place**, containing a statue of a famous person. Below is a list of some famous people from the history of French-speaking places. Choose one famous person from the list. Then complete the research card with information about him or her.

1. Charlemagne
2. Jeanne d'Arc
3. Louis XIV
4. Jacques Cartier
5. Cavelier de La Salle
6. Le marquis de La Fayette
7. Napoléon Bonaparte
8. Marie Antoinette
9. Clovis
10. Blaise Pascal
11. Louis Pasteur
12. Marie Curie
13. Victor Hugo
14. Auguste Rodin
15. Léopold Senghor
16. Vercingétorix
17. Édith Piaf
18. Charles de Gaulle
19. Aimé Césaire
20. George Sand

Town Square Statue Research Card

La statue: Nom
Date de naissance (jour, mois, année) (*Birthdate*)
Ville et pays
Profession
Accomplissements importants (*Important accomplishments*)
L'histoire du pays pendant sa vie (*History of the country during his or her lifetime*)

G. UNE STATUE D'UNE PERSONNE CÉLÈBRE

You learned that in the center of many French-speaking cities, **la place** has a statue of a famous person (**une statue d'une personne célèbre**). At the base of **la statue**, there is often a plaque that gives visitors information about that person.

In the picture frame below, put a drawing or other picture of the **personne célèbre** you selected for your research in Activity F. Use your research notes to complete the plaque.

H. LA POSTE

One of the most important buildings you need to be able to find is the post office (**la poste**). All of your family and friends back home will want postcards and letters (**lettres**). Here are some useful phrases (**expressions utiles**) for the post office. Do you already know any of them? Translations are shown in the second chart. Practice these **expressions utiles** with your teacher.

Bonjour	Madame Monsieur Mademoiselle			
Je voudrais	envoyer acheter	une carte postale un aérogramme un timbre	par avion aux États-Unis	s'il vous plaît
Merci				
Au revoir	Madame Monsieur Mademoiselle			

Hello	Ma'am Sir Miss			
I'd like	to send to buy	a postcard an airmail letter a postage stamp	by airmail to the United States	please
Thank you				
Good-bye	Ma'am Sir Miss			

How would you ask for a stamp to send a postcard to a friend in the United States? Working with a partner, use the **expressions utiles** to create a dialogue between yourself and a postal employee.

I. UNE CARTE POSTALE

Below is **une carte postale**. Use it to write to your family in the United States. Tell them about some of the things you're doing. Summarize what you've learned during your homestay about **la ville et la famille**. Then address **la carte postale**. Don't forget **le timbre**!

timbre

J. LA CARTE

You've had a busy day exploring your new surroundings. You mailed your **carte postale**. This evening, your homestay family is taking you to a restaurant (**un restaurant**) for dinner. You want to be prepared for this new experience. Can you read the menu (**la carte**) on the next page? Go over it with a partner. Do you know what to order? Look for cognates, such as **salade** (*salad*) and **saumon** (*salmon*). Place a check mark (√) next to any items on the menu that are *unfamiliar* to you. Your teacher will help you understand them.

La carte

Les entrées
Salade composée (tomates, riz, maïs, oignon)
Crudités (tomates, betteraves, céleri)
Salade de tomates
Salade de concombres
Soupe à l'oignon
Soupe du jour
Pâté maison
Saucisson

Les plats principaux
Poulet rôti/frites
Bifteck/frites
Poulet à la normande
Bœuf bourguignon
Poulet provençal
Porc tourangeau
Côtelettes de porc grillées
Poisson du jour
Saumon grillé
Brochette de bœuf

Les desserts
Mousse au chocolat
Crème caramel
Tarte aux fraises
Gâteau au chocolat
Glace (vanille, fraise, chocolat)

Les boissons
Coca, limonade, Orangina, eau minérale
Café, thé, jus d'orange, jus d'ananas,
   jus de pamplemousse

Can you read **la carte**? For more practice, categorize foods from **la carte** into the columns below.

SALADE	**POULET**	**BŒUF**	**POISSON**

Now, decide what you would like to order for dinner (**le dîner**). Circle your choices on **la carte** on the opposite page. **Prêt(e)? Allons au restaurant!**

K. VOUS DÉSIREZ?

You've decided what you'd like to eat. Do you know how to order these items in **le restaurant**? The **serveur/serveuse** (*waiter/waitress*) says, "**Vous desirez?**" (*What would you like?*) You answer, "**Je voudrais** (*I'd like*)_____ ." Practice these two phrases with your teacher. Then, working with a partner, practice ordering the foods you have selected on **la carte** in Activity J. Use the dialogue below as a model.

Serveur/Serveuse: **Vous desirez?**

Toi: **Je voudrais** _____ , _____ ,

_____ et _____ , **s'il vous plaît.**

L. JEU DE LA VILLE

With some help, you've found **la poste, la banque**, and some other places in **la ville**. Let's see if you can find your way around **la ville** to do things on your own. Play this city game (**jeu de la ville**) with a group of two to four classmates. Your teacher will give each team a stack of cards, a game board, colored tokens, and a die. The object of the game is to reach **la confiserie** with as few cards as possible. Follow these directions carefully. The picture on the game board tells you what you find in **la confiserie**.

1. Each player:
   - Selects a colored token as his or her own
   - Places his or her token at the start, marked **Commence ici** (*Begin here*)
   - Draws six cards with pictures of things to see or buy
   - Rolls the die to see who goes first (The lowest number goes first. If it's a tie, then those players roll again.)

2. Player A tosses the die and moves his or her token the number of spaces indicated.

3. If Player A lands on a space that matches a shop or place of interest shown on one of the cards in his or her hand, Player A discards that card to a throw-away pile.

4. If none of Player A's cards matches the space, he or she must draw another card.

5. Play then passes to Player B.

6. The game continues until one player reaches **la confiserie** and is declared the winner.

Here's some more information to help you play. Your teacher will practice these phrases with you before you start. These are also **expressions utiles** when you're playing other games.

Recule de 2 cases.	*Go back two spaces.*
Avance de 2 cases.	*Advance two spaces.*
Tu perds un tour.	*You lose your turn.*
C'est encore ton tour.	*Take another turn.*

M. MON JOURNAL

You've learned about your host city. Did you enjoy your meal at the restaurant? In your journal, write anything you'd like to write about your experiences under **Nouveaux renseignements**. You may also want to include information you learned about a famous French-speaking person. Select five to ten new French words or phrases from this Element. Write them under **Mes mots.** Under **Mon dessin**, put a drawing of the famous person you studied, something you saw in the city, or your favorite food from your dinner at the restaurant.

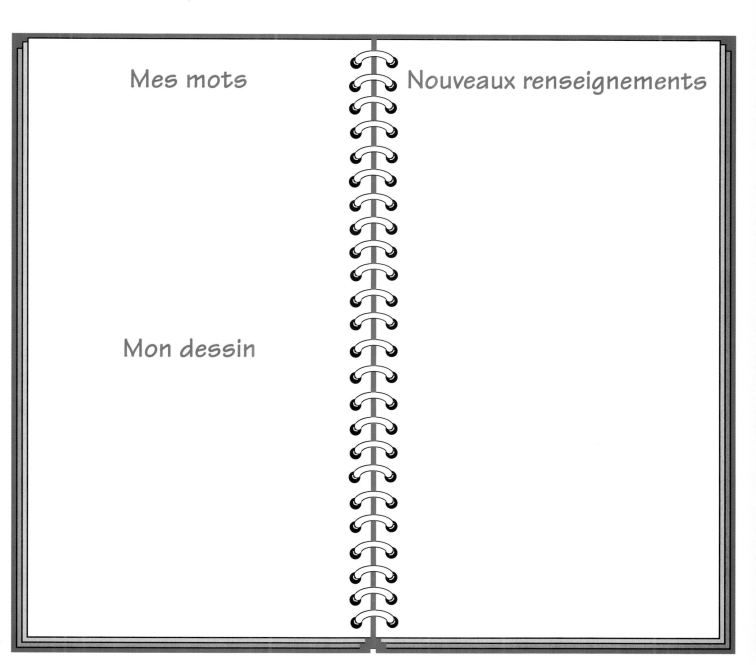

Mes mots

Nouveaux renseignements

Mon dessin

PERSPECTIVE

Attending school and participating in extracurricular activities helps homestay students understand life in their homestay country. In this Element, you get acquainted with your new school and decide which clubs you want to join. In addition, you have an opportunity to describe your hometown school to your new classmates. **Allons-y!**

Nom _____
Emploi du temps: Cours moyen 2

Heure	lundi	mardi	mercredi	jeudi	vendredi	samedi
8h	français	anglais	espagnol	éd. physique	maths	maths
9h	français	français	espagnol	histoire	maths	anglais
10h	maths	sciences	dessin	français	anglais	français
11h	anglais	maths	maths	français	français	français
12h	DÉJEUNER			DÉJEUNER		
13h	histoire	informatique		maths	éd. physique	
14h	éd. physique	éd. physique	PAS DE COURS	anglais	informatique	PAS DE COURS
15h	sciences	dessin		sciences	géographie	
16h	informatique	géographie		musique	sciences	

Année _____ **Niveau** (*Grade level*) _____ **Élève** _____

Clubs — jour

le club international — lundi

photographie — mardi

tennis — mercredi

peinture — jeudi

Préférences

1ère _____ tennis

2e _____ club international

3e _____ peinture

4e _____ photographie

A. LES COURS

During your homestay, you attend courses (**les cours**) with your host brother and sister. What are **les cours** you can select? Here is a list of **les cours** available to you in your homestay school. Listen carefully while your teacher says them in French. Can you guess what they are in English? Practice repeating the names of **les cours** after your teacher. Then write the English equivalents in the blanks. Notice that the French word for *the* appears in front of each subject and also that the subject names are not capitalized.

Example:

l'anglais   *English*

1. la musique   _____

2. la géographie   _____

3. l'histoire   _____

4. le français   _____

5. les maths   _____

6. l'éducation physique _____

7. le dessin   _____

8. l'allemand   _____

9. les sciences   _____

10. l'informatique   _____

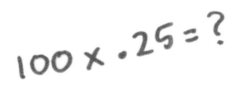

B. LES CLUBS

Unlike students in the United States, students in the French-speaking world normally do not participate in organized school sports. Instead, they participate in clubs (**les clubs**), which are scheduled late in the school day. During your homestay, you may also participate in **les clubs**. Look at the list below. Do you have any of these extracurricular activities or clubs in your school? If so, circle the names of the clubs you have. Now, practice saying all the names with your teacher. Then write the English equivalents in the blanks. (Remember, you do not use *the* in English.)

Example:

la natation *swimming*

1. le club international _____

2. le débat _____

3. la photographie _____

4. le cyclisme _____

5. le tennis _____

6. le théâtre _____

7. le volley _____

8. la peinture _____

9. les jeunes astronautes _____

10. la gymnastique _____

C. MES PRÉFÉRENCES

Now that you know something about the available clubs and activities in your homestay school, you can register to participate. Below is a registration form. Complete the top part with your personal information. (Remember to use your homestay **adresse** and **téléphone**.) Then look at the list of clubs. Select four and list them in the order of your interest. All of **les clubs** meet at 5:00 P.M., except on Wednesdays and Saturdays when they meet after lunch. Write the names of your four clubs and the days they meet on the appropriate lines.

Inscription aux clubs

Nom _____

Adresse _____

_____

Téléphone _____

Âge _____

Niveau (*Grade level*) _____

Club	Jour	Club	Jour
le club international	lundi	le théâtre	mercredi
le débat	lundi	le volley	jeudi
la photographie	mardi	la peinture	jeudi
le cyclisme	mardi	les jeunes astronautes	vendredi
le tennis	mercredi	la gymnastique	samedi

Mes préférences

1ère _____

2e _____

3e _____

4e _____

 Note French uses the small **-er (-ère)** or **-e** after a number to indicate rank order. In English, we use the following numerical abbreviations: 1st, 2nd, 3rd, 4th, etc.

D. L'EMPLOI DU TEMPS

You've selected your extracurricular activities. Now it's time to complete your schedule. Review the classes and clubs available at your host school, as shown on pages 109 and 110. List the classes you want to take in the appropriate blanks on the schedule below. Indicate the clubs you decided to join in the blanks following **Clubs**.

Nom _____			Emploi du temps _____			
Heure	lundi	mardi	mercredi	jeudi	vendredi	samedi
8 h						
9 h						
10 h						
11 h						
12 h	DÉJEUNER			DÉJEUNER		
13 h						
14 h						
15 h						
16 h						

Année _____ **Niveau** _____ **Élève** _____

Clubs: Préférences
1ère _____
2e _____
3e _____
4e _____

E. PAPIER, CRAYONS ET LIVRES

Now that you have chosen the classes you want to take during your homestay, you need to buy some school supplies. In many parts of the world, students buy items such as paper and pencils (**le papier et les crayons**) or books (**les livres**) in a bookstore (**la librairie**) or a stationery store (**la papeterie**). Is this different where you live? Discuss the differences, if any, with your teacher and classmates.

_____ 1. un cahier	_____ 5. une feuille de papier	_____ 9. une calculatrice
_____ 2. un crayon	_____ 6. un taille-crayon	_____ 10. une gomme
_____ 3. un stylo	_____ 7. une règle	_____ 11. un feutre
_____ 4. un livre	_____ 8. un sac à dos	_____ 12. du papier cartonné

Above is a list of some basic school supplies. Listen and repeat as your teacher pronounces them. Try to guess the meanings of the words. Check your predictions with your teacher. Do the meanings of some of the words surprise you?

 Note **Un** and **une** mean *a*. The two forms match the **le** and **la** forms for the word *the*. The word **du** means *some*.

Working with a partner, review the words listed above and match them to the objects in the classroom picture. Write the letter of each picture by the appropriate French word. When you are finished, check with your teacher to see how well you have done.

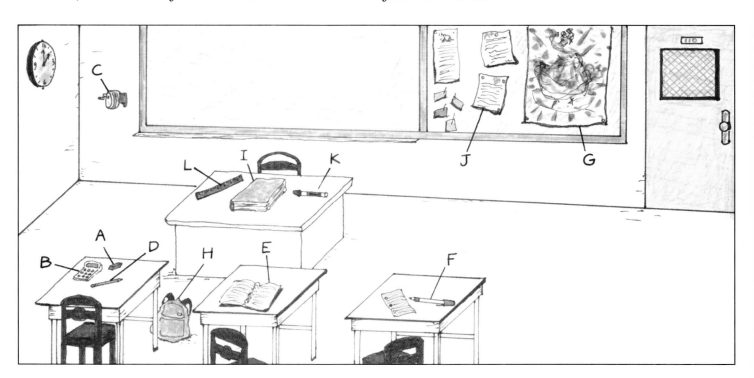

F. EXERÇONS-NOUS!

Here are some scrambled French words for school courses and school supplies. Working with a partner, see how quickly you can unscramble the words. After you have unscrambled each one, write it in the blank that follows it. Then write the letter of each picture after the appropriate French word.

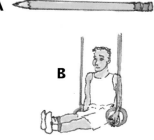
A

B

C

1. GQYNMTEAUIS

D

2. VILER

E

3. EESNICCS

4. ÉEHGAGPIOR

F 100 × .25 = ?

5. YCRNAO

G

6. MMGOE

7. SFÇAARNI

H

8. TMAHS

G. QUELS COURS ET QUELS CLUBS EST-CE QUE TU PRÉFÈRES?

Now you know the French words for a number of school courses and clubs (**les cours et les clubs**). Which ones are the most popular? Let's take a poll in French. Look at the sentences below. You need to use them to take your poll. Listen to your teacher model the sentences, then repeat them. Practice them with a partner. **Prêt(e)?**

Questions: **Quel cours est-ce que tu préfères?** *Which class do you prefer?*
Quel club est-ce que tu préfères? *Which club do you prefer?*

Answer: **Je préfère _____.** *I prefer _____.*

Below is a list of school subjects and clubs. Use the sentences you have just learned to take a poll of 15 classmates. If your classmates do not know the French phrases, you can teach them what to say. For example,

you ask: they answer:

Quel cours est-ce que tu préfères? **Je préfère les sciences.**
Quel club est-ce que tu préfères? **Je préfère le tennis.**

Find out each person's favorite subject and favorite club. Tally the results and record the totals on the correct line below.

Les cours

_____ l'anglais
_____ le français
_____ l'espagnol
_____ l'histoire
_____ la géographie
_____ les maths
_____ la musique
_____ les sciences
_____ l'éducation physique
_____ le dessin
_____ l'informatique

Les clubs

_____ la natation
_____ le débat
_____ la photographie
_____ le cyclisme
_____ le tennis
_____ le théâtre
_____ le volley
_____ le club international
_____ les jeunes astronautes
_____ la gymnastique

When you have completed your poll and tallied the responses, report your findings to the class. You may do this as an oral or written report, or in a chart, graph, or any other format you select.

H. COMMENT EST TON ÉCOLE?

What is your school like? (**Comment est ton école?**) You have been asked to develop a project that tells what school is like in your hometown. You will then present your project to your new French-speaking classmates. Here are seven steps to help you. Read through the steps before you begin. Your teacher will give you a checklist to use as you work on your project. Check off (√) each step as you complete it. The first step has four phases. **Bonne chance!**

STEP 1: BRAINSTORM IDEAS AND OUTLINE YOUR PRESENTATION.

Phase 1. Working with a partner, brainstorm information you want to share about your school. What topics would be interesting to your new French-speaking classmates? Write all of your ideas on a sheet of paper.

Phase 2. By yourself, review all of your ideas for topics. Select those you want to use in your project. Write them in the cells on the idea map below. You may add more cells, if you wish.

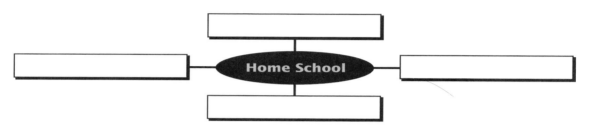

Phase 3. Next, decide on the order in which you want to present your topics. Write them in that order on the index card below. After listing the topics, discuss with your partner what specific information you want to give about each one. Then write your ideas next to the main topics on the card.

1.

2.

3.

4.

Phase 4. Finally, choose the exact way you plan to present your project. You may wish to make a poster and explain it, or you may prefer to compose a written report. You can select any form of presentation that interests you. Your teacher will give you some other suggestions and help you decide on the format you want to use.

Write the kind of project you plan to present here: _____

STEP 2: MAKE A SHOPPING LIST FOR YOUR SUPPLIES.

Look at the list of supplies on page 113. What do you need for your project? You need to go shopping (**faire des courses**) for supplies. Put them on the shopping list below. If you need items that are not on the list, consult an English-French dictionary or ask your teacher.

Ma liste

_____   _____

_____   _____

_____   _____

_____

STEP 3: DESIGN THE ART FOR YOUR PROJECT.

You've planned your project and you've bought your supplies. You need to get started. Pictures, photographs, and drawings make a project more interesting and informative. Think about how you can illustrate each of the ideas from your idea map and index card outline. Cut out or draw pictures or use photos. Organize them on a poster or incorporate them in another way into the presentation of your project.

STEP 4: LABEL EACH DRAWING OR PICTURE IN FRENCH.

Label each illustration using as much French as you can. Remember that neither you nor your French-speaking classmates are completely fluent in each other's language. Use simple French to present your ideas. Sometimes you can use just one word. For example, to label a picture of your friends at lunch, you can write **mes amis(amies)—le déjeuner**. You can use the word **Emploi du temps** to label a copy of your schedule and fill in the subjects in French. (Refer to page 109 if you need a reminder.)

STEP 5: PRACTICE PRESENTING YOUR PROJECT.

Practice your presentation with your partner. Your partner takes the role of your French-speaking classmates. Use as much French as possible. Try to be interesting and entertaining. Ask your partner for suggestions to improve your presentation. Then give your partner a chance to practice and you can give him or her your suggestions.

STEP 6: PRESENT YOUR PROJECT.

Give your practiced and improved presentation to the class. Use the notes from your outline, your illustrations, and the helpful suggestions from practice with your partner. Remember to include as much French as you can!

STEP 7: GRADE YOUR PROJECT.

In your host school, students may not receive the same kinds of grades (A, B, C, etc.) as you do in the United States. The grading system in many French-speaking schools (**écoles francophones**) is from 1 to 20. Your project will be graded using a scale of 1 to 20. Below is your host teacher's grading scale. Can you translate the 1 to 20 scale into the grading system used in your school?

Evaluation			Equivalent in the U.S.A. System
18–20	Très Bien	90–100%	_____
13–17	Bien	80–89%	_____
10–12	Moyen	70–79%	_____
8–9	Insuffisant	60–69%	_____
0–7	Très insuffisant	0–59%	_____

What do you think your grade should be for your project? _____

Why?_____

_____

Does your teacher agree? _____

Why or why not? _____

_____

I. MON JOURNAL

You've had a busy time learning about the similarities and differences between your home school and your host school. In your journal, write a review of the new information you learned in this Element. Write about **tes cours et tes clubs** under **Nouveaux renseignements**. Remember those new key words and phrases in French! Write them under **Mes mots.**

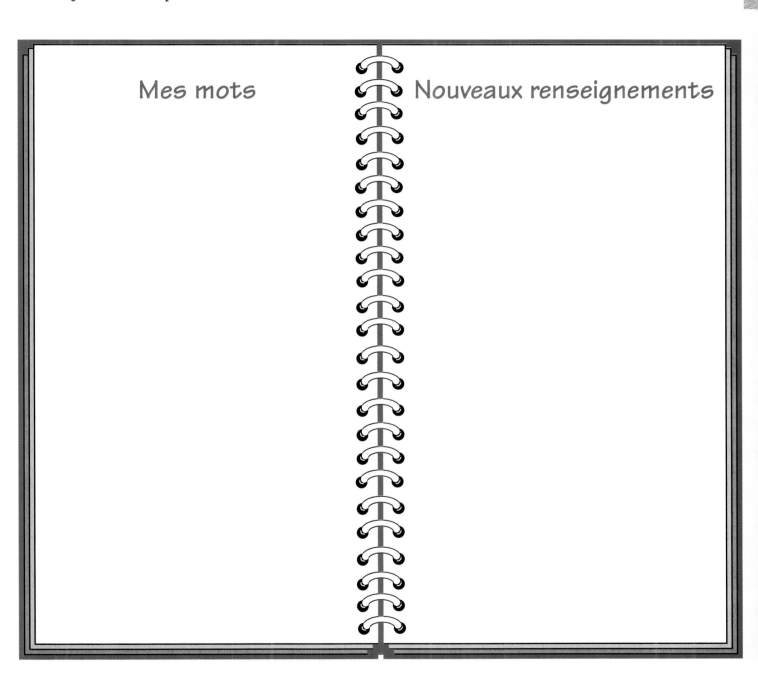

Mes mots

Nouveaux renseignements

11

SIGHTSEEING

PERSPECTIVE

Throughout your home-stay, you've learned about families, schools, and individual interests. In this Element, you explore interesting places in the French-speaking world. **Bon voyage!**

À VISITER

le Musée National du Louvre
lundi, mercredi
9h–21h45
jeudi–dimanche
9h–18h
fermé le mardi

le Centre Georges-Pompidou
lundi, mercredi–vendredi
12h–22h
samedi, dimanche
10h–22h
fermé le mardi

À VISITER

la Cathédrale Notre-Dame de Paris
lundi–dimanche
8h–19h

la Tour Eiffel
lundi–dimanche
hiver: 10h–23h
été: 9h30–0h

Euro Disneyland
lundi–vendredi
9h–19h
samedi, dimanche
9h–21h

EXCURSIONS

Tour #1:
Louvre, Tour Eiffel et Centre Pompidou. Le tour part de l'hôtel le mardi à 9h30.

Tour #2:
Euro Disneyland. Le tour part de l'hôtel le jeudi et le samedi à 8h30.

A. VILLES INTÉRESSANTES

Travel experiences build memories for a lifetime. If France is your homestay country, you will want to see everything you can during your visit. As a special side trip, you may be able to visit a number of famous cities, towns, and villages throughout France. These cities are located in various historical regions of France called **provinces**. You may also be interested in visiting cities in other French-speaking countries. Listed below are some major cities in France and in several other French-speaking countries.

Listen carefully while your teacher says them in French. Now, repeat them after your teacher. Can you guess where any of them are? (HINT: You may have learned about some of these cities if you studied Element 1.) Working with a partner, write your ideas in the blanks. When you are finished compare your answers with your classmates' answers. The first city is easy, **n'est-ce pas** (*isn't it*)?

CITY	COUNTRY/REGION
1. Paris	_____
2. Nouméa	_____
3. Marseille	_____
4. Cap-Haïtien	_____
5. Dakar	_____
6. Bruxelles	_____
7. Strasbourg	_____
8. Papeete	_____
9. Avignon	_____
10. Limoges	_____
11. Montréal	_____
12. Berne	_____
13. Cayenne	_____
14. Kairouan	_____
15. Abidjan	_____

B. OÙ SONT LES VILLES DU MONDE FRANCOPHONE?

Now that you know where some key French-speaking cities are, let's find out more about those regions and countries. This information can be found in a number of different ways. Choose two of the cities on the last page. Working alone or with a partner, consult materials such as encyclopedias, atlases, computer databases, and other references in your library or media center. Ask the librarian, your teachers, or other resource persons to help you. You might also call or visit a local travel agent to find more information. After doing your research, prepare a report about the cities you selected. Use your imagination! Your report may be written, oral, or visual. Consider making a collage of pictures or photographs that you can show and describe to your class.

On the card below write the names of several cities that your classmates described in their reports. Include some information you would like to remember about each of them.

C. MOYENS DE TRANSPORT

You've discovered some **villes intéressantes**. Let's plan to visit one of them. To take a tour (**une excursion**), you can use different methods of transportation (**moyens de transport**). Listen while your teacher says the forms of transportation in French and then asks you to repeat them. It's easy to guess what they mean in English, isn't it?

la motocyclette   l'autobus   le métro   l'auto   le train

You may also want to walk (**marcher**). Listen again as your teacher says the words. Then practice them with a partner. Now you know **les moyens de transport**. **Allons-y!**

 In many French-speaking countries, the cost of owning and operating a private automobile is very expensive. People are much more likely to walk or use bicycles, motorbikes, or public transportation.

What **moyen de transport** is the most popular? Working with a partner, conduct **une enquête** (*a survey*). Ask ten of your classmates to tell you their first (**premier**) and second (**deuxième**) choices of transportation. Each time a person answers, put a **1er** or **2e** following the **moyen de transport** they choose. When you're finished with the survey, report your findings to your teacher and your classmates.

Classmate	1	2	3	4	5	6	7	8	9	10
la motocyclette	☐	☐	☐	☐	☐	☐	☐	☐	☐	☐
l'autobus	☐	☐	☐	☐	☐	☐	☐	☐	☐	☐
le métro	☐	☐	☐	☐	☐	☐	☐	☐	☐	☐
l'auto	☐	☐	☐	☐	☐	☐	☐	☐	☐	☐
le train	☐	☐	☐	☐	☐	☐	☐	☐	☐	☐

Totals:

la motocyclette   1er _____   2e _____   l'autobus   1er _____   2e _____

le métro   1er _____   2e _____   l'auto   1er _____   2e _____

le train   1er _____   2e _____

D. LE MÉTRO? QU'EST-CE QUE C'EST?

What is the subway? (**Qu'est-ce que c'est que le métro?**) If you go sightseeing in a large city (**une grande ville**) such as Paris, you'll probably take **le métro**. Each of the following sentences has French words in bold print. These are important words (**mots importants**) when you take **le métro**. Can you guess what these **mots importants** mean in English? Read the sentences quietly to yourself. Now, as your teacher reads each sentence aloud, write your prediction of the English meaning in the blank following the French term.

1. You begin by going through **l'entrée** (_____).

2. To ride **le métro** (_____), you need to buy **un ticket** (_____).

3. You buy **ton ticket** (_____) at a place called **un guichet** (_____).

4. Metro lines or routes are color coded and named for the final stop at the end of the line. That is your **direction** (_____).

5. If you need to change lines along the way, you make **une correspondance** (_____). (HINT: In this sentence, **correspondance** is not a cognate!)

6. The **stations de métro** (_____) are named for major sites or famous people.

7. When you arrive at your **station** (_____), get off the metro, look for the signs, and leave through **la sortie** (_____).

8. Once you pass through **une sortie** (_____), you need a new **ticket** (_____) to reenter.

Your teacher will read the sentences again to help you and your classmates check your responses.

How did you do? Check (√) one.

Bien (*Well*) _____   **Comme ci, comme ça** (*So-so*) _____   **Mal** (*Badly*) _____

Make corrections to your predictions as necessary.

> *Note* The Paris **métro** is one of the best-developed subway systems in the world. There are eighteen lines. Route maps (**les plans de métro**) are posted throughout the cars (**les voitures**) and in the stations.

E. UN TOUR DANS LE MÉTRO

Look at the Paris metro map and answer the questions for each of the following situations.

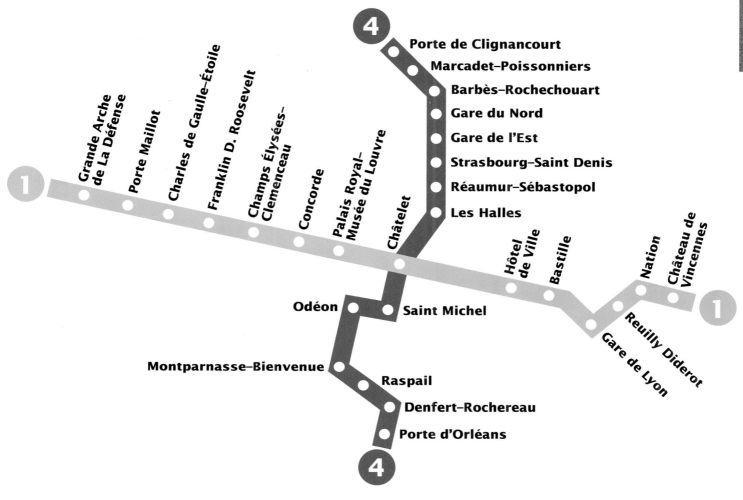

You are at your hotel, which is near the **Palais-Royal** metro stop on line 1. You want to go to see the **Arc de Triomphe** at metro station **Charles-de-Gaulle-Étoile**.

1. Do you need to make **une correspondance**? **Oui** or **non**? _____
2. Are you traveling **direction Grande Arche de la Défense** or **Château de Vincennes**? Circle one.
3. How many **stations de métro** do you pass? _____

Now use both metro line 1 and metro line 4. You've finished your sightseeing at the **Arc de Triomphe**, and you want to visit the gardens and the area near **Saint-Germain-des-Prés**.

4. Are you traveling **direction Grande Arche de la Défense** or **Château de Vincennes**? Circle one.
5. At which **station** do you need to make a **correspondance**?_____
6. What is your new **direction** on this line, **Porte d'Orléans** or **Porte de Clignancourt**? Write the **direction** here. _____

Congratulations! **Félicitations!** Now you can find your way around **la ville** like an experienced traveler.

F. QUEL TEMPS FAIT-IL?

What's the weather like? (**Quel temps fait-il?**) The weather is an important factor when planning **une excursion**. Look at the following pictures. Each one depicts a certain kind of weather. Below each picture is the French expression you use to describe that kind of weather. Listen and repeat each expression after your teacher.

Il fait du soleil.

Il pleut.

Il fait du vent.

Le ciel est couvert.

Il fait froid.

Il fait chaud.

Practice these phrases first with your teacher and then with a partner. Now your teacher will say one of these expressions. Point to the picture that illustrates the kind of weather your teacher is describing. Next, complete the sentence below with a French expression for weather.

Je préfère quand (*I prefer when*) _____.

Why is this your favorite kind of weather?_____

_____

G. UNE COMPARAISON DE TEMPÉRATURES

We frequently like the weather because we like the temperature (**la température**). In the United States, we measure **la température** in Fahrenheit. Your homestay country measures **la température** on the Celsius scale. Look at the thermometer on this page. It shows a quick way to understand Celsius and compare it to Fahrenheit.

Here are some average monthly temperatures for your homestay city. They are given in Celsius. Using the thermometer, change the Celsius temperatures to approximate Fahrenheit temperatures. Write the new temperatures in the blanks. How does each temperature compare with those of your hometown in the United States? Place a check (√) next to the best response.

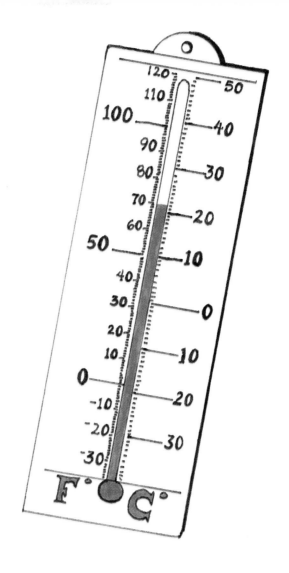

1. janvier   8°C _____ °F   Higher _____   Lower _____   About the same _____

2. mars   14°C _____ °F   Higher _____   Lower _____   About the same _____

3. juin   25°C _____ °F   Higher _____   Lower _____   About the same _____

4. août   30°C _____ °F   Higher _____   Lower _____   About the same _____

5. septembre   22°C _____ °F   Higher _____   Lower _____   About the same _____

6. novembre   12°C _____ °F   Higher _____   Lower _____   About the same _____

H. LES ACTIVITÉS ET LA TEMPÉRATURE

La température and other weather conditions often help us decide which activities to plan. Below are the French words for some of the **activités** that you can enjoy during your homestay. Can you guess the English equivalent of each? Some of them were presented in earlier Elements. Working on your own or with a partner, write your predictions in English on the line under the French word or phrase. Try to guess the meaning of any new words or phrases. Look for cognates. Your teacher will verify the answers with you. Make necessary corrections. Then write the letter of each picture in front of the French form it illustrates.

_____ 1. faire des courses

_____

_____ 2. faire du canoë

_____

_____ 3. nager

_____

_____ 4. faire du cheval

_____

_____ 5. regarder une cassette video

_____

_____ 6. aller au cinéma

_____

_____ 7. jouer au base-ball

_____

_____ 8. faire du vélo au parc

_____

_____ 9. marcher

_____

Now complete these sentences with three **activités** you like to do and your **activité préférée**.

J'aime _____ , _____ et _____.

Ce que je préfère, c'est (*What I like best is*) _____

I. FAISONS DES PROJETS!

You know some French expressions for activities. **Faisons des projets!** (*Let's make plans!*) Form a group of two or three students. Below is the weather report for the week. Given these weather conditions, what kind of activities are appropriate? Decide which **activités** your group wants to do each day. Write them on the lines following **Activités** at the bottom of the chart. If you studied page 41 or 47 in Element 4, you learned the French expressions for some other activities. You may wish to add some of those activities to this list. (If you think of other things you want to do but don't know the French words, consult a dictionary or ask your teacher to help you.)

ACTIVITÉS

JOUR	TEMPS	TEMPÉRATURE	ACTIVITÉS
lundi	Le ciel est couvert.	7°C	_____ _____
mardi	Il fait du soleil.	15°C	_____ _____
mercredi	Il pleut.	26°C	_____ _____
jeudi	Il fait du vent.	33°C	_____ _____
vendredi	Il pleut.	30°C	_____ _____
samedi	Il fait chaud.	35°C	_____ _____
dimanche	Il fait froid.	3°C	_____ _____

J. MON JOURNAL

Record what you learned about **les villes intéressantes** in your journal. Using as much French as you can, write about **une excursion** and **les transports**. Write this under **Nouveaux renseignements**. What do you remember about taking **le métro**? You also learned how to talk about the weather in French. Select five to ten new words or expressions from this Element. Write them under **Mes mots**. Draw a picture of your **activité préférée** or something to depict **une ville intéressante** under **Mon dessin**.

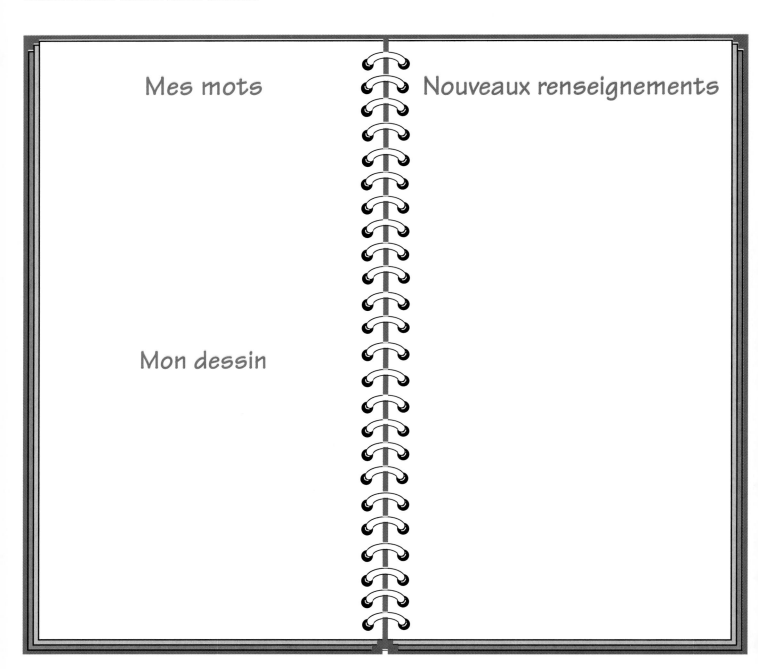

Mes mots

Nouveaux renseignements

Mon dessin

Street musicians in Guadeloupe

Cafe in a small town in Alsace, France

An exhibit of paintings by Marc Chagall in France

12   A BIRTHDAY PARTY

PERSPECTIVE

You have been busy during your homestay. You've been sightseeing and attending a new school. You are enjoying meeting new French-speaking friends, and they have invited you to a birthday party. In this Element, you help plan the party, buy a birthday present, and make a birthday card. Of course, you also go to the party! Have a good time!
Amuse-toi bien!

A. L'INVITATION

Look at this invitation (**l'invitation**). You're invited to a birthday party! Each line on the invitation begins with a word that asks a question. Can you guess the meaning of these question words in English? Your teacher will review each one with you as you predict its English meaning. Now listen and repeat the words after your teacher. Then, practice saying them with a partner. These words can be very useful when you want to ask for information.

B. UNE CARTE

You are invited to a birthday party for Philippe and are going to design a card (**une carte**). Below are some French phrases that are appropriate to use in a birthday card. Listen while your teacher pronounces them. Some of them have an exclamation mark (**!**). These phrases should be said with enthusiasm! Now, listen again and repeat the phrases after your teacher.

Finally, decide which phrases to use on your **carte** for Philippe. Your teacher will give you the materials you need to make **la carte**. Plan, design, and create **une carte** to take to the party.

C. DES IDÉES POUR UN CADEAU

Now, let's go buy a present! **Allons acheter un cadeau!** Look below at the list of possible gifts (**cadeaux**) you could buy for Philippe. Do you know what they are in English? Work with a partner to review the items on the list. Now, listen and repeat them in French after your teacher. Then, match the letter of each picture on the right with the corresponding French word on the left. When you are finished, verify your responses with your teacher.

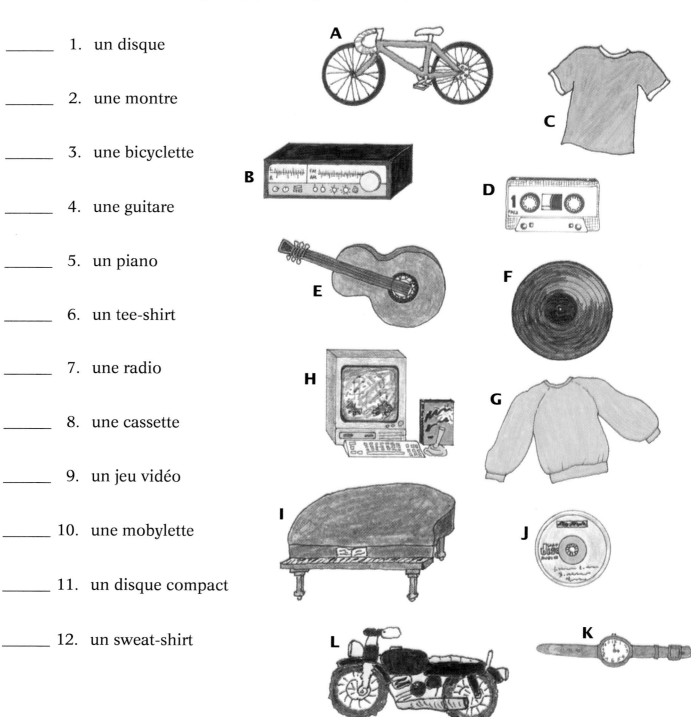

_____ 1. un disque

_____ 2. une montre

_____ 3. une bicyclette

_____ 4. une guitare

_____ 5. un piano

_____ 6. un tee-shirt

_____ 7. une radio

_____ 8. une cassette

_____ 9. un jeu vidéo

_____ 10. une mobylette

_____ 11. un disque compact

_____ 12. un sweat-shirt

Next, on the scrap of paper to the right, write a list of four ideas for Philippe's **cadeau**. Pretend you can spend as much money as you want. Any idea is acceptable. Be creative!

Can you think of any other **cadeaux pour Philippe**? With your classmates, brainstorm other possibilities. List them in the web below. If you don't know the French for the choices you've made, consult an English-French dictionary or ask your teacher. When you are finished, share your ideas with the class.

D. DES NOMBRES UTILES POUR FAIRE DES COURSES

Let's go shopping! (**Allons faire des courses!**) You want to review **les nombres utiles pour les courses** (*the useful numbers for shopping*). You've already learned to count from 1 to 100 in French. Practice counting with your teacher or a partner. If you're working with a partner, take turns counting after every ten numbers. **Prêt(e)? Un, deux, trois...**

To help you **faire des courses**, your teacher will dictate prices to you ranging from 1 to 100. Cross out each number as you hear it. Your teacher will give you the correct answer after dictating the number. Check your memory! **Prêt(e)?**

| 12 | 24 | 37 | 48 | 59 | 60 | 65 | 70 | 79 | 81 | 93 | 100 |

Since you have unlimited funds for shopping, you want to be able to say numbers greater than 100. Look at the numbers below. Listen while your teacher says them in French. Do you recognize any of these numbers?

100	**cent**	800	**huit cents**
200	**deux cents**	900	**neuf cents**
300	**trois cents**	1.000	**mille**
400	**quatre cents**	10.000	**dix mille**
500	**cinq cents**	100.000	**cent mille**
600	**six cents**	1.000.000	**un million**
700	**sept cents**		

E. C'EST COMBIEN?

C'est combien? (*How much is it?*) You're ready to buy **un cadeau** for Philippe's birthday party. When you go shopping, you need to ask the price. To do so, you ask, **"C'est combien?"** or **"Combien coûte _____?"** Listen as your teacher asks the question. Then repeat it.

You know that Philippe likes music and you think you might buy a CD (**un disque compact**). Listen while your teacher asks in French, "How much does a CD cost?" Then repeat the question. Now, write the question by filling in the missing letters in French:

Combien c__ __ __ __ u__ d__ __ __ __ __ __ c__ __ __ __ __ __ __ ?

F. LE PRIX

In France, money is measured in **francs**. The numbers representing the price (**le prix**) will usually be followed by the abbreviation **F**.

Your teacher will give you an envelope of cards representing price tags. Arrange the price tags in order from the smallest amount to the largest amount. Your teacher will say the French word for a gift and then give its price. Write the French term for each item on the line under the drawing and place the price tag next to it.

For example, your teacher will say: **Une cassette coûte cent francs (100 F).**

You write **une cassette** on the line under the correct drawing and place the **100 francs** price tag next to it.

une cassette

1.
_____

2.
_____

3.
_____

4.
_____

5.
_____

6.
_____

7.
_____

8.
_____

9.
_____

10.
_____

11.
_____

12.
_____

G. LE JEU DES COURSES

The object of the shopping game (**le jeu des courses**) is to buy all the items on your shopping list and have money to spare. This is a timed activity. When the timer stops, the shopper who has found the most items on his or her list and has the most money left wins.

Banker's preparation (your teacher or a student volunteer plays the role of the banker):

1. Have available one envelope for each student (shopper) in the class.

2. Place **2.500 francs (F)** into each envelope as follows: three **500 F** notes, five **100 F** notes, six **50 F** notes, five **20 F** notes, eight **10 F** coins, and four **5 F** coins.

3. Give each shopper an envelope.

Shopper's preparation:

First, review and practice all of your numbers.
Next, practice asking for what you would like to buy, saying:

Je voudrais _____ **, s'il vous plaît.**

Then, practice asking how much an item costs by saying:

Combien coûte _____**?**

Ready to play? **Prêt(e) à jouer?** Follow these steps:

1. Prepare a shopping list.

   • Select any five items from the list in Activity F on page 137.

   • Write the five items on your shopping list.

   • Review the entire list to make sure you know the vocabulary.

   • Practice the words on the list with a partner.

2. From your teacher, select five cards with pictures of items on them. These will be your trading cards of items to sell. On the back of each card, write:

   • The French term for the item.

   • The price you are asking for the item.

3. Get your money envelope from the banker.

Each shopper will have the following:

- an envelope containing **2.500 F**
- a shopping list of five items to buy
- five trading cards of items to sell

Let's go shopping! (**Allons faire des courses!**)

1. Circulate around the room asking classmates for an item on your shopping list saying:

   Je voudrais _____ **, s'il vous plaît**.

2. If the person you approach does not have the item, he or she says:

   Je n'en ai pas.

   If he or she has the item, you ask how much it costs:

   Combien coûte _____?

   He or she will answer:

   Ça coûte _____ **francs**.

3. If the price is reasonable, pay for the item with your money and take the card. If the price is too high, try finding someone else who has the same item for a lower price.

4. Move on to the next person, repeating the same dialogue.

5. When the time is up, count your purchases and your remaining cash. Be prepared to name the items you have purchased and tell, in French, how much money you have left.

H. LE FAST-FOOD

After all that shopping, you think, "I'm hungry!" (**J'ai faim!**). There are fast-food restaurants throughout the French-speaking world and they become more popular each year. You stop to get a snack (**un casse-croûte**). Look at the menu. Then, get ready to order your food!

HAMBURGER	LAIT
HAMBURGER AU FROMAGE	JUS D'ORANGE
POULET	COCA-COLA
FILET DE POISSON	FANTA
FRITES (PETITE/MOYENNE/ GRANDE PORTION)	
CAFÉ	CITRON PRESSÉ
THÉ (CHAUD, GLACÉ)	MILK-SHAKE

Note   **Citron pressé** means *lemonade*. Another drink, called **limonade**, is flavored carbonated water.

If you studied Element 9, you learned how to order food from a waiter or waitress in a regular restaurant. Fast-food restaurants are more informal, but the expressions you use to talk to the employees will be similar. Look at the dialogue below. Listen and repeat the expressions after your teacher.

hamburger	au fromage
poulet	
filet de poisson	
frites (petite/moyenne/grande portion)	
café	
thé (chaud, glacé)	
lait	
jus d'orange	
Coca-Cola	Fanta
milk-shake	
limonade	
citron pressé	

    Employé(e):   **Vous désirez?**
        Client(e):   **Je voudrais _____ , s'il vous plaît.**
    Employé(e):   (*Write order on form. Then repeat order aloud.*)
        Client(e):   **Oui, merci.**
          or   **Non, je voudrais** (*repeat order*), **s'il vous plaît.**

Working with a partner, use the **expressions** and the menu to practice ordering your snack. Take turns playing the role of the **client(e)** and the **employé(e)**. Remember to say your order clearly.

Note   The best-known fast-food restaurant in France is McDonald's, nicknamed **Macdo**. There are also Burger King restaurants on the famous **Champs-Élysées**. The major French fast-food restaurant chain is called **Le Quick**.

I. UNE FÊTE D'ANNIVERSAIRE

You've completed your shopping for **le cadeau** and stopped for **un casse-croûte**. Your **carte** is completed. It's time to plan the party (**la fête**). Everyone loves **une fête**, especially to celebrate **un anniversaire**. To plan the party, follow these steps:

1. With your class and your teacher, select

   - a birthday party theme

   - the kinds of planning committees you need. Each committee should be responsible for planning one aspect of the party—invitations, food, entertainment, decorations, etc.

2. Divide the class into these committees.

3. Each committee develops its plan. (Remember that your shopping lists, invitations, menu, etc., need to be in French.)

4. Give each committee member a number (1, 2, 3, 4, etc.).

5. Send all number 1's (one person per committee) to form an information group. Do the same with all number 2's, all number 3's, etc.

6. In each information group, share the plans from your original committee. Ask for suggestions, and make sure that all the plans fit together to make a great party.

7. Go back to your original planning committee. Share new suggestions from the information group with your original team members. Adjust your plans, if necessary.

Review your shopping lists and make your invitations.

Prêt(e)? Let's start the party!
Commençons la fête!

J. L'ANNIVERSAIRE DE PHILIPPE

You're dressed for **la fête**. Your **cadeau** is wrapped. Take your camera! You want photos for your journal. Look again at **l'invitation** in Activity A on page 133. **À quelle heure est la fête?**
À _____. You still have time to go to the florist (**le/la fleuriste**).

 It is customary to buy some flowers (**des fleurs**) for the person who is hosting a party.

As you arrive, you notice that everyone is talking, laughing, or dancing. Look at the picture of Philippe's **fête** below. What do you see? To describe what you see at **la fête**, you say:

Je vois _____.   *I see ____.*

Il y a _____.   *There is (are) ____.*

Work with a partner. Look at the picture. In the time your teacher gives you, identify in French as many objects, people, and activities as you can. Write the French words or phrases in the idea web.

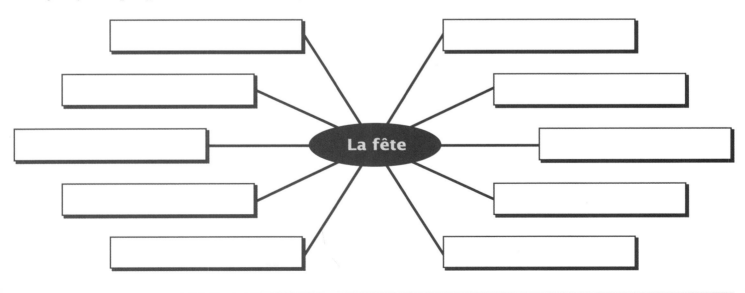

K. MON JOURNAL

You've been busy planning, shopping for, and attending Philippe's party. Write a few lines in your journal under **Nouveaux renseignements** to remember these important events. Select five to ten new French words or **expressions importantes** from this Element. Write them under **Mes mots**. Under **Mon dessin**, sketch a copy of the birthday card you made. It was **superbe**!

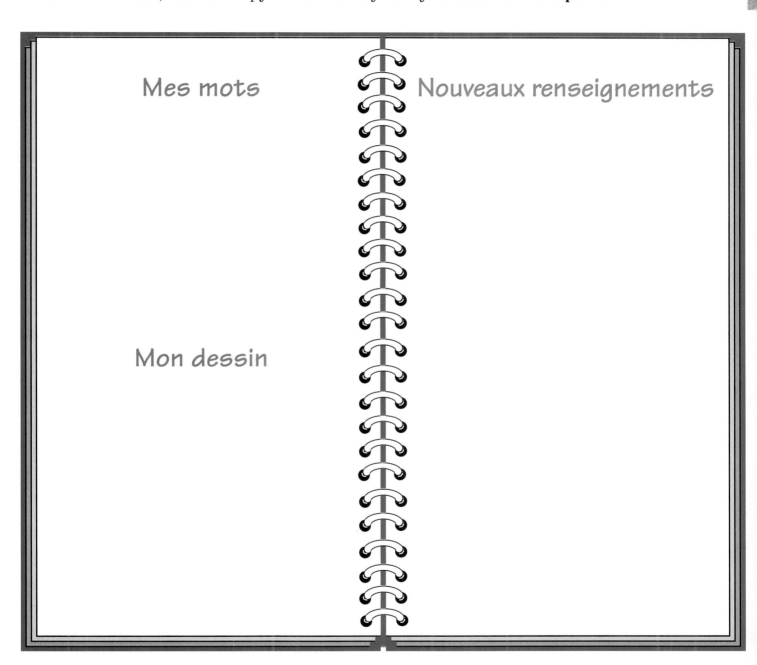

Mes mots

Nouveaux renseignements

Mon dessin

SOUVENIRS D'UN BON VOYAGE

PERSPECTIVE

You enjoyed your homestay experience. You met your host family and participated in their daily life. You learned about your homestay country as you attended school, rode public transportation, and went sightseeing, shopping and to a birthday party with friends. Now, it's time to go home! Too bad! (**Quel dommage!**)

In this Element, you construct a scrapbook of memories (**souvenirs**) of your homestay experience. You want each section of the scrapbook to show a different part of your homestay. This will be nice to share with your family and friends at home! Your scrapbook will also help you review the French you have learned. Your teacher will give you an Organization and Assessment Grid. You and your teacher will use this grid to assess your project. As you organize **tes souvenirs**, keep the criteria on the grid in mind.

A. MA VIE FRANCOPHONE

Your family and friends and your French teacher want to learn about your life **(ta vie)** during your homestay. In your scrapbook, describe the time you spent with your host family and new friends. Include things you want to remember about your new school, your favorite sites, and your activities. To show your teacher how much French you've learned, use as much French as possible in your descriptions. Put in a lot of **photos** and **dessins**, too. Think about what was especially interesting during your homestay that you want to share with everyone at home. In the space below, design a cover for your scrapbook. **Allons-y!**

B. LA FAMILLE

Your scrapbook is a perfect way to share information about your host family. Start the scrapbook by showing **la famille.** Place a picture or a drawing of them in the space labeled **La famille**. Write some information about them below the picture.

To help you begin, some sentence starters are written below. Don't limit yourself to these sentence starters, however. Be creative! There may be many things you'd like to share about **la famille** using **photos** or **dessins**. Be sure to label your pictures in French (**en français**). If you need help, use a dictionary or ask your classmates or your teacher.

La famille

Dans la famille, il y a _____ personnes.

Ils s'appellent _____

_____

_____

Ils sont _____
                    (describe their personalities)

_____

_____

You also want to show **la maison** where you lived. In the space labeled **La maison**, put a picture of the house you stayed in during your homestay. Write information about **la maison** below the picture.

La maison

Mon adresse est _____

_____

Mon numéro de téléphone est le _____

Ma maison est _____
(color and size)

Dans la maison, il y a _____
(describe rooms, furnishings)

_____

_____

C. MON ÉCOLE

You want your family, friends, and teachers to know about your homestay school and the clubs you joined. In the space labeled **Mon emploi du temps**, include a schedule of your classes. Along with the schedule, write information about **l'école**.

Mon emploi du temps

Mon école s'appelle _____

_____

Mon école est à _____
                                        (city)

Mes cours sont _____
                                        (classes)

_____

_____

_____

Include **un dessin** or **une photo** in the space to show something about the **clubs** you joined. Then write information about the clubs.

Les clubs

Mes clubs s'appellent _____

_____

_____

J'aime mieux _____

(*your favorite club*)

_____

D. LES VILLES INTÉRESSANTES

You can't wait to tell everyone about **les villes intéressantes** that you explored during your stay. Place a photo or drawing of one of the sightseeing highlights of the cities you investigated in each space labeled **Ville intéressante**. Give historical details or other basic information about each city below its picture. Remember to use your notes from Element 11. Use the sentence starters if you want, but don't limit yourself to them alone. You may want to include additional information about these places. If you need help, use a dictionary or ask your classmates or your teacher.

Ville intéressante

Cette ville s'appelle _____

Cette ville est au/en _____
(country name)

La ville est _____
(describe the city)

_____

Détails intéressants: _____

_____

_____

_____

Ville intéressante

Cette ville s'appelle _____

Cette ville est au/en _____
(country name)

La ville est _____
(describe the city)

_____

Détails intéressants: _____

_____

_____

_____

E. LES TRANSPORTS

Your friends will be very impressed by your ability to travel independently during your homestay. This scrapbook page helps you tell them or show them how you were able to get around. Give some information about **le métro**. Include **un dessin** of a metro map showing the stops. Use the **mots importants** you learned for traveling on **le métro**. When you describe one station, give some historical information about the famous person or location for which it is named.

Le métro

Le métro a _____ stations.
     (number)

To ride the **métro**, you need to buy a _____ at a place

called a _____. You can transfer to another **métro** line

by making a _____. When you arrive at your stop,

you get off the **métro** and leave through _____.

One **station** is named _____,
                        (name of famous person or location)

because _____

_____.

F. FAISONS DES COURSES

Your homestay also taught you about shopping in another country. Your French teacher and your classmates are curious about what students your age in French-speaking countries buy and how much these items cost. On this page of your scrapbook, include information about your shopping. Show **une photo** or **un dessin d'un cadeau pour Philippe**. Label it in French.

Faisons des courses

Voilà une photo (un dessin) de mon cadeau pour Philippe.

Mon cadeau pour Philippe est _____.

Ça coûte_____.

Autres achats que j'ai faits (*Other purchases I made*).

_____

_____

_____

_____

G. LES RENSEIGNEMENTS ET LES CONSEILS

You have learned a lot of new things during your homestay. Think about **les renseignements et les conseils** (*the information and advice*) you want to share with other students who are going to participate in the homestay next year. Include **des dessins**, **des photos**, and written information on these two pages of your scrapbook.

Les renseignements et les conseils

Les renseignements _____

_____

_____

_____

Les conseils _____

_____

_____

_____

Les renseignements et les conseils

Les mots importants _____

_____

_____

_____

_____

_____

_____

H. BON VOYAGE!

You are finished with your scrapbook. Now it's time to prepare for the trip back home. You have your scrapbook of **souvenirs** and some **cadeaux pour ta famille**. Think of how much fun it will be to share your scrapbook as well as all of your experiences with your family and friends. Your classmates and teacher are sure to be impressed with all of the French you know! You've had a chance truly to explore the language. Are you ready to continue learning more French? **Bonne chance!**

This certainly has been a **bon voyage!**

Calèche in Montreal, Canada

Uzès market in Provence, France

Butcher shop in France

■ GLOSSARY

A

à at, to
  À bientôt. See you soon.
  à côté (de) beside, next to
  à (cinq) heures at (five)
    o'clock
  à l'aéroport at the airport
  à l'école to school
  à quelle heure? at what
    time?
abricot, un apricot
accomplissement, un
  accomplishment
achat, un purchase
acheter to buy
actif(-ive) actif
activité, une activity
adresse, une address
aérienne: une ligne aérienne
  airline
aérogramme, un airmail
  letter
aéroport, un airport
affectueux(-euse) affec-
  tionate
africain(e) African
âge, l' (*m.*) age
  Quel âge as-tu? How old
    are you?
ai: j'ai I have
  j'ai (douze) ans I'm
    (twelve) years old
  j'ai chaud I'm hot
  j'ai faim I'm hungry
  j'ai froid I'm cold
  j'ai soif I'm thirsty
  je n'ai pas de... I don't
    have . . .
  je n'en ai pas I don't have
    any
aimable nice, kind
aime: J'aime... I like . . .
  J'aime mieux... I prefer...,
    I like . . . better
  J'aime... le mieux I like . . .
    the best
  Je n'aime pas... I don't
    like . . .
album, un photo album
algérien(ne) Algerian

allemand, l' (*m.*) German
  (language)
aller to go
  aller à l'école to go to
    school
  aller au cinéma to go to a
    movie
  aller au concert to go to a
    concert
  **aller au match (de foot-
    ball)** to go to a (soccer)
    game
  aller au parc to go to the
    park
Allons-y! Let's go!
ambitieux(-euse) ambitious
américain(e) American
Amérique du Nord, l' (*f.*)
  North America
Amérique du Sud, l' (*f.*)
  South America
ami(e), un(e) close friend
amuser: s'amuser to have fun
  Amuse-toi bien! Have fun!
  Amusez-vous bien! Have
    fun!
an, un year
  j'ai (douze) ans I'm
    (twelve) years old
ananas, un pineapple
anglais, l' (*m.*) English
  (language)
animal, un (*pl.* **animaux**)
  animal
  animaux domestiques
    domestic animals, pets
année, une year
  année scolaire school
    year
anniversaire, un birthday
  Bon anniversaire! Happy
    birthday!
  Joyeux anniversaire!
    Happy birthday!
août August
appartement, un apartment
appelle(nt):
  il/elle s'appelle
    his/her/its name is
  ils/elles s'appellent their
    names are

  je m'appelle my name is
appétit, un appetite
  Bon appétit! Enjoy your
    meal!
après-midi, un afternoon
  de l'après-midi in the
    afternoon, P.M.
argent, l' (*m.*) money
arrive: j'arrive I arrive
arrivée, l' (*f.*) arrival
arrogant(e) arrogant
art, l' (*m.*) art
as: tu as you have
Asie, l' (*f.*) Asia
assez enough
astronaute, un(e) astronaut
attends: j'attends I'm waiting
  for
au (*pl.* **aux**) to the
aujourd'hui today
au revoir good-bye
aussi also, too
auto, une car
autobus, un bus
autre other
  un(e) autre another
aux to the
  aux États-Unis to the
    United States
Avance de deux cases.
  Advance two spaces.
avant before
avec with
  avec plaisir with pleasure
avenue, une avenue
aviation, l' (*f.*) aviation
avion, un airplane
  par avion by airmail
avoir to have
avons: nous avons we have
avril April

B

bagages (*m. pl.*) luggage
baguette, une long loaf of
  French bread
baignoire, une bathtub
banane, une banana
banque, une bank

base-ball, le baseball
basket-ball, le basketball
bavard(e) talkative
beau (belle) beautiful
beaucoup a lot
  beaucoup de a lot of
belge Belgian
belle (*see* **beau**)
betterave, une beet
beurre, le butter
beurré(e) buttered
bien well; fine, great, good
  elles sont bien they're
    great
  très bien very good, very
    well
bientôt soon
  À bientôt! See you soon!
Bienvenue! Welcome!
bienvenue, une welcome
bifteck, un steak
bijouterie, une jewelry store
biologie, la biology
bise, une kiss
blanc (blanche) white
bleu(e) blue
blouson, un jacket
bœuf, le beef (meat)
  bœuf bourguignon beef
    Burgundy (stewed in
    red wine)
boisson, une beverage
bon(ne) good
  Bon appétit! Enjoy your
    meal!
  Bonne chance! Good
    luck!
  Bon voyage! Have a good
    trip!
bonjour good morning,
  hello
boulevard, un boulevard
boutique, une boutique
brochette de bœuf, une beef
  on a skewer
brosse, une brush
  brosse à dents toothbrush
brun(e) brown
bureau, un desk; office
  bureau de poste post
    office

C

ça:
    Ça va? How are you?
    Ça va. I'm fine.
    Ça va bien. Everything's fine.
cadeau, un present, gift
café, le coffee
café, un café; (cup of) coffee
cahier, un notebook
calculatrice, une calculator
calme quiet
canadien(ne) Canadian
canapé, un sofa
carotte, une carrot
carte, la menu
carte, une card
    carte d'anniversaire birthday card
    carte postale postcard
casse-croûte, un snack
cassette, une (audio)cassette
    cassette vidéo videocassette
catégorie, une category
cathédrale, une cathedral
ce (cet, cette) this
    ce que what
    Ce que je préfère, c'est... What I prefer is . . .
ceinture, une belt
célèbre famous
céleri, le celery
cent hundred
    deux cents two hundred
    cent mille a hundred thousand
central(e) central, in the middle
centre, le center
c'est it is
    C'est combien? How much is it?
cette (*see* ce)
chaîne stéréo, une stereo system
chaise, une chair
chambre, une bedroom
champignon, un mushroom
chance, la luck
    Bonne chance! Good luck!
change, un money exchange
changer to change; to exchange (money)
chat, un cat
château, un castle
chaud(e) warm, hot
    il fait chaud it's warm

chaussette, une sock
chaussure, une shoe
chef, un chef
chemise, une (man's) shirt
chemisier, un (woman's) shirt, blouse
chèque, un check
    chèque de voyage traveler's check
cher (chère) expensive; dear
    c'est cher it's expensive
    cher monsieur dear Sir
cheval, un horse
cheveux (*m. pl.*) hair
chez at
    chez moi at my house
    chez vous at your house, home
    près de chez moi near my house
chien, un dog
chiffre, un numeral
    la date en chiffres the date in numerals
chinois(e) Chinese
chocolat, le chocolate
    la mousse/un gâteau au chocolat chocolate mousse/cake
chose, une thing
ciel, le sky
cinéma, le movies
cinéma, un movie theater
cinq five
cinquante fifty
citron, un lemon
    citron pressé lemonade
classe, une classroom
client(e), un(e) customer
club, un club
Coca, le Coca-Cola
combien? how much?
    C'est combien? How much is it?
    Combien coûte... ? How much is . . . ?
    Combien de... ? How many . . . ?
comme ci, comme ça so-so
Commence ici. Begin here.
Commençons! Let's start!
    Commençons la fête! Let's start the party!
comment how
    Comment allez-vous? How are you?
    Comment dit-on... en Français? How do you say . . . in French?

    Comment est ton école? What is your school like?
commun: en commun in common
comparaison, une comparison
composé(e) composed, mixed
    une salade composée mixed salad
comprendre to understand
concert, un concert
concombre, un cucumber
    une salade de concombres cucumber salad
confiserie, une candy store
confiture, la jelly
conseil, un advice
copain, un friend, pal (male)
copine, une friend, pal (female)
correspondance, une transfer, change of train lines
côté, un side
    à côté de beside, next to
côtelette, une cutlet
    côtelettes de porc grillées grilled pork cutlets
couche:
    il/elle se couche he/she goes to bed
    je me couche I go to bed
couleur, une color
coup: un coup de téléphone a phone call
coupe cut
couper to cut
courageux(-euse) courageous
cours, un course, class; grade level
    cours de (maths) math course
    en cours in class
    en cours moyen 2 in the 7th grade
court: un court de tennis tennis court
coûte costs
    Combien coûte... ? How much does . . . cost?
couvert(e) cloudy
    le ciel est couvert it's cloudy
crayon, un pencil
crème, la cream
    crème caramel caramel cream

crudités (*f. pl.*) raw vegetables
cuisine, une kitchen
cuisinière, une stove
cyclisme, le cycling

D

dames (*f. pl.*) women
dans in, at
    dans ma famille in my family
    dans mon école in, at my school
danse, une dance
danser to dance
date, une date
    date de naissance birthdate
d'autres others
    d'autres choses other things
de of, from, in
    de l'après-midi in the afternoon
débat, un discussion, debate
décembre December
déjà already
    Tu as déjà... You already have . . .
déjeune eat(s) lunch
déjeuner to eat lunch
déjeuner: le petit déjeuner breakfast
délicieux(-euse) delicious
demain tomorrow
demande, une application
    demande de passeport passport application
demi(e) half
    et demi(e) half past, 30 minutes past the hour
dentifrice, le toothpaste
départ, le departure
derrière behind
des from; of; some
    des États-Unis from the United States
description, une description
désirer to wish, to want
    Vous désirez? What would you like?
dessert, un dessert
dessin, un drawing
détroit de Gibraltar, le Strait of Gibraltar
deux two
deuxième second
devant in front of

devoir, un homework
dimanche, (le) Sunday
dîne eat(s) dinner, supper
direction, une direction
disquaire, un music store
disque, un record
  disque compact compact disque
distance, une distance
dit:
  il/elle dit he/she says
  on dit you say
dix ten
dix-huit eighteen
dix-neuf nineteen
dix-sept seventeen
dollar, un dollar (bill)
dominos, les (*m.*) dominoes
donner to give
d'où from where
douane, la customs
douanier(-ière), un(e) customs officer
douche, une shower
douze twelve
droit straight
  tout droit straight ahead
  Va tout droit. Go straight ahead.
droite, la right
  à la droite to the right
du of the; in the; from the; some
  du matin in the morning
  du soir in the evening
  du papier some paper

E

eau, une water
  eau minérale mineral water
école, une school
  mon école my school
écouter to listen
  écouter de la musique to listen to music
éducation physique, l' (*f.*) physical education
église, une church
égoïste selfish
égyptien(ne) Egyptian
élève, un(e) pupil, student
elle she
elles they (feminine)
embrasser to kiss
  je t'embrasse I kiss you
emploi du temps, un schedule

employé(e), un(e) employee
en in; by; to
  en autobus by bus
  en face de across from
  en français in French
  en quel mois... in what month . . .
  en ville to town, downtown
enchanté(e) delighted
  Je suis enchanté(e) de faire votre connaissance. It's nice to meet you.
encore again; still
  C'est encore ton tour. It's still your turn. Take another turn.
enquête, une survey
enseigne, une sign (on stores and buildings)
entrée, une entrance
enveloppe, une envelope
envoyer to send
espagnol, l' (*m.*) Spanish (language)
espagnol(e) Spanish
Essayons! Let's try!
est: il/elle est he/she/it is
Est-ce que... ? (Is it true that) . . . ?
et and
États-Unis, les (*m. pl.*) United States
étiquette, une tag
  étiquette à bagages luggage tag
étudiant(e), un(e) student
étudier to study
  J'étudie le français. I study (am studying) French.
Europe, l' (*f.*) Europe
évier, un (kitchen) sink
examen, un test
excursion, une excursion, (sightseeing) trip
Exerçons-nous! Let's practice!
expression, une expression
extroverti(e) extroverted

F

face: en face de across from
facile easy
  C'est facile, non? It's easy, isn't it?
faim, la hunger

j'ai faim I'm hungry
faire to do, make
  faire de la photo take pictures
  faire des achats/courses to go shopping
  faire du canoë to go canoeing
  faire du cheval to go horseriding
  faire du ski to go skiing
  faire du vélo to ride a bicycle
  faire un voyage to take a trip
  il y a beaucoup à faire there's a lot to do
fais: je fais mes devoirs I do my homework
faisons let's do, make
  Faisons des projets! Let's make plans!
fait
  il fait chaud it's hot
  il fait du soleil it's sunny
  il fait du vent it's windy
  il fait froid it's cold
  il fait ses devoirs he does his homework
famille, une family
fast-food, le fast food
fatigué(e) tired
  je suis fatigué(e) I'm tired
fauteuil, un armchair
faux (fausse) false
Félicitations! (*f.pl.*) Congratulations!
fête, une party
feuille, une sheet
  feuille de papier sheet of paper
feutre, un marker
février February
fiche, une form
  fiche de renseignements personnels personal information form
fille, une girl
fin, une end
Finis... Finish . . .
fleur, une flower
fleuriste, un(e) florist
fleuve, un river
fois, une time, occurrence
  une fois one time, once
football, le soccer
  football américain (American) football
frais (fraîche) fresh
fraise, une strawberry

une tarte aux fraises strawberry pie
franc, un franc
français, le French (language)
français(e) French
francophone French-speaking
  le monde francophone French-speaking world
frère, un brother
frigo, un fridge, refrigerator
frites (*f. pl.*) French fries
froid, le cold
  il fait froid it's cold
fruit, un fruit

G

gagner to win
garçon, un boy
gare, une train station
gâteau, un cake
  gâteau au chocolat chocolate cake
gauche, la left
  à la gauche to the left
généreux(-euse) generous
géographie, la geography
glace, la ice cream
glacé(e) cold, iced
  un thé glacé iced tea
golfe, un gulf
  Golfe du Mexique Gulf of Mexico
gomme, une eraser
grand(e) big, large; tall
grillé(e) barbecued, grilled
gris(e) grey
guichet, un ticket window
guitare, une guitar
gymnastique, la gymnastics

H

haïtien(ne) Haitian
hamburger, un hamburger
  hamburger au fromage cheeseburger
heure, l' (*f.*) time
  À quelle heure? At what time?
  il est une heure it's one o'clock
  il est (deux) heures it is (two) o'clock
  Quelle heure est-il? What time it is?

heure, une hour
 les heures de pointe rush hour
histoire, l' (*f.*) history
hockey, le hockey
hommes (*m. pl.*) men
hôpital, un hospital
horloge, une clock
hors-d'œuvre, un appetizer
hôtel, un hotel
huit eight

I

ici here
idée, une idea
il he, it
 il faut it is necessary
 il y a there is/are
ils they (masculine)
impatience, l' (*f.*) impatience
important(e) important
impression, une impression
inscription, une registration
indécis(e) indecise
indépendant(e) independent
informatique, l' (*f.*) computer sciences
installation, l' (*f.*) arrangement of furniture and household items in a home
insuffisant(e) insufficient, unsatisfactory
 très insuffisant very unsatisfactory
intelligent(e) intelligent
intéressant(e) interessant
international(e) international
 un club international international club
interview, une interview
invitation, une invitation
italien(ne) Italian

J

jaloux(-ouse) jealous
janvier January
japonais(e) Japanese
jaune yellow
je I
 j'ai I have
 je m'appelle... my name is . . .
 je suis I am
jean, un blue jeans
jeu, un game

jeu des courses shopping game
jeu vidéo video game
jeudi, (le) Thursday
jeune young
joli(e) pretty
jouer to play
 jouer au football to play soccer
 jouer de la musique to play music
 Prêt(e) à jouer? Ready to play?
jour, un day
 jours de la semaine days of the week
journal, un journal; newspaper
journaliste, un(e) journalist
journée, une day
 une journée avec... a day with . . .
joyeux(-euse) joyful, merry
 Joyeux Noël! Merry Christmas!
juillet July
juin June
jupe, une skirt
jus, un juice
 jus d'ananas pineapple juice
 jus de citron lemon juice
 jus d'orange orange juice
 jus de pamplemousse grapefruit juice

K

karaté, le karate

L

la the (feminine)
là here; there
 ...n'est pas là! . . . is not here!
lac, un lake
lait, le milk
laitue, la lettuce
lampe, une lamp
lavabo, un (bathroom) sink
le the (masculine)
lecture, la reading
les the (plural)
lettre, une letter
lève:
 il/elle se lève he/she gets up
 je me lève I get up

librairie, une bookstore
librairie-papeterie, une book and stationery store
limonade, une flavored carbonated soda drink
lire to read
liste, une list
lit, un bed
livre, un book
loin (de) far (from)
lundi, (le) Monday
lycée, un high school

M

ma my
madame (Mme) Ma'am, Mrs.
mademoiselle (Mlle) Miss
magasin, un store
mai May
mais but
maison, une house, home
mal badly, poorly
malade ill, sick
Manche, la English Channel
mange eat(s)
manger to eat
 manger au restaurant to eat in a restaurant
marcher to walk
mardi, (le) Tuesday
marocain(e) Moroccan
marron brown, chestnut
mars March
mathématiques (maths) (*f.pl.*) mathematics (math)
matin, un morning
 du matin in the morning, A.M.
meilleur(e) best
 meilleurs vœux/souhaits best wishes
mer, une sea
 mer des Antilles Caribbean Sea
 mer Rouge Red Sea
 mer Méditerranée Mediterranean Sea
merci thank you
mercredi, (le) Wednesday
mère, une mother
mes (*pl.*) my
métro, un metro, subway
mets: Mets (la radio) dans... Put (the radio) in . . .
mexicain(e) Mexican
midi noon
 il est midi it's noon
milk-shake, un milk-shake

mille thousand
 mille fois a thousand times
million, un a million
minuit midnight
 il est minuit it's midnight
mobylette, une moped
moi me
moins less; before (the hour)
 moins le quart quarter to, 15 minutes before the hour
mois, un month
mon my
monde, le world
 monde francophone French-speaking world
monnaie, la change
monsieur (M.) Sir, Mr.
montre, une watch
monument, un monument
morceau, un piece
mot, un word
 mot nouveau new word
motocyclette, une motorcycle
mousse au chocolat, la chocolate mousse
moyen, un means, method
 moyen de transport method of transportation
musée, un museum
 musée du Louvre Louvre Museum
musique, la music

N

n' (*see* **ne**)
nager to swim
naissance, une birth
 la date de naissance birthdate
natation, la swimming
nature, la nature
ne not
 n'est-ce pas? isn't it?, doesn't it?
 N'oublie pas... Don't forget . . .
 n'est-ce pas? isn't it?, doesn't it?
neuf nine
niveau, un grade level
noir(e) black
nom, un name
 nom de famille last name
nombre, un number

non no; not

  non? right?, don't you agree?

  non plus either

nord, le north

  Amérique du Nord North America

note, une note

N'oublie pas... Don't forget . . .

nous we, us

nouvelle (*see* **nouveau**)

nouveau (nouvelle) new

novembre November

nuit, une night

numéro, un number

O

obéissant(e) obedient

océan, un ocean

  océan Atlantique Atlantic Ocean

  océan Indien Indian Ocean

octobre October

œuf, un egg

oignon, un onion

  la soupe à l'oignon onion soup

oiseau, un bird

omelette, une omelet

on dit you say

onze eleven

orange orange

orange, une orange

  jus d'orange orange juice

Orangina, une orange soda

organisation, une organization, plan

ou or

où where

  d'où from where

  Où est/sont... ? Where is/are . . . ?

  Où se trouve(nt)... ? Where is/are . . . ?

oublie: N'oublie pas... Don't forget . . .

oui yes

P

pain, le bread

palais, un palace

pamplemousse, un grapefruit

  un jus de pamplemousse grapefruit juice

panneau, un (street) sign

pantalon, un (pair of) slacks

papeterie, une stationery store

papier, le paper

  du papier cartonné cardboard, poster board

  une feuille de papier sheet of paper

par by

  par avion by airmail

parapluie, un umbrella

parc, un park

pardon excuse me

parent, un parent

parents, les parents

paresseux(-euse) lazy

parler to talk, to speak

  parler au téléphone to talk on phone

  parler avec des amis to talk with friends

passé: Le voyage s'est bien passé? Did the trip go well?

passeport, un passport

pâté maison, le paté (specialty of the house)

pâtisserie, une bakery (store)

pays, un country

peigne, un comb

peinture, la painting

pendant during

père, un father

perdu(e): Je me suis perdu(e). I got lost.

perds: Tu perds un tour. You lose a turn.

personne, une person

personnel(le) personal

perspective, une perspective

petit(e) small

  petit déjeuner, le breakfast

peu, un a little

photo, une photo

photographie, la photography

piano, un piano

pièce, une room

  pièces de la maison rooms of the house

pizza, une pizza

place, une (town) square

plaisir, le pleasure

plan, un map

  plan de métro metro map

plat, un meal, dish

  plat principal main dish

pleut: il pleut it's raining

pluie, la rain

poisson, un fish

pont, un bridge

porc, le porc

  porc tourangeau pork as cooked in Tours or Touraine

porte, une door; entrance

portion, une serving

poste, la post office

poulet, le chicken

  poulet à la normande chicken Normandine

  poulet provençal chicken Provencal

  poulet rôti roasted chicken

pour for

pourquoi why

  pourquoi pas why not

préfère: je préfère (quand) ... I prefer (when) . . .

préféré(e) favorite

préférence, une preference

premier (première) first

  le premier janvier the first of January

prend(s):

  il/elle prend (le petit déjeuner) he/she takes/eats (breakfast)

  je prends I take; I eat

prénom, un first name

préparation, une preparation

  préparation du voyage travel preparation

près (de) near, close (to)

  près de chez moi near my house

pressé(e) squeezed

  un citron pressé lemonade

prêt(e) ready

principal(e) main

prix, un price

professeur, un professor

  professeur de français French professor

profession, une occupation

projet, un plan

public (publique) public

pull-over, un sweater

Q

quand when

quarante fourty

quart, un quarter

  et quart quarter after, quarter past, fifteen minutes past the hour

quartier, un neighborhood

quatorze fourteen

quatre four

quatre-vingt-dix ninety

quatre-vingts eighty

quatre-vingt-un eighty one

quatrième fourth

quel (quelle) what, which

  Quel cours est-ce que tu préfères? Which class do you prefer?

  Quel dommage! What a shame!, Too bad!

  Quel temps fait-il? What's the weather like?

  Quelle heure est-il? What time is it?

quelle (*see* **quel**)

Qu'est-ce que c'est? What is it?

  Qu'est que c'est que (la liberté)? What is (freedom)?

qui who

quinze fifteen

quitter to leave

R

radio, une radio

raquette (de tennis), une (tennis) racquet

réclamation, une claim

Recule de deux cases. Go back two spaces.

regarder to watch

  regarder la télé watch TV

région, une region, area

règle, une ruler

remercie: je vous remercie thank you

rempli(e) filled

remplir to fill (out)

  remplir une fiche to fill out a form

renseignement, un information

réponse, une response, answer

restaurant, un restaurant

rester to stay

rien nothing

riz, le rice

robe, une dress

rose pink

rôti(e) roasted

un poulet rôti roasted chicken
rouge red
rue, une street
russe Russian

S

sa his/her
   sa vie his or her life(time)
sac, un bag
   sac à dos, un backpack
salade, une salad; lettuce
   salade de concombres cucumber salad
   salade de tomates tomato salad
salle à manger, une dining room
salle de bains, une bathroom
salon, un living room
Salut! Hi!
salutations (*f. pl.*) greetings, regards
samedi, (le) Saturday
sandwich, un sandwich
saucisson, un sausage, salami
saumon, le salmon
sciences (*f. pl.*) science(s)
seize sixteen
sel, le salt
semaine, une week
sénégalais(e) Senegalese
sentiment, un sentiment, feeling
   mes sentiments les meilleurs my best regards
sept seven
septembre September
serveur, un waiter
serveuse, une waitress
serviette, une towel
short, un (pair of) shorts
signature, une signature
s'il vous plaît please
six six
ski, le skiing; ski
   ski nautique water skiing
sœur, une sister
soif, la thirst
   j'ai soif I'm thirsty
soir, un evening
   du soir in the evening
soixante sixty
soixante-dix seventy
soleil, le sun
   il fait du soleil it's sunny

son his/her
sont are
   ils/elles sont they are
sortie, une exit
souhait, un wish
   Meilleurs souhaits pour ton anniversaire! Best wishes for your birthday!
soupe, la soup
   soupe du jour soup of the day
souvenir, un souvenir
   souvenirs memories
spontané(e) spontaneous
sport, le sports
station, une station, stop
   station de métro subway station
statue, une statue
   statue de la Liberté Statue of liberty
stylo, un (ballpoint) pen
sucre, le sugar
sud, le south
   Amérique du Sud South America
suis: je suis I am
   je suis de... I am from . . .
   je suis malade I'm ill/sick
suisse Swiss
sur on; about
sweat-shirt, un sweatshirt

T

table, une table
taille-crayon, un pencil sharpener
tarte, une pie
   tarte aux fraises strawberry pie
tartine, une open-face sandwich
   tartine au chocolat sandwich with chocolate
taxi, un taxi, cab
tee-shirt, un T-shirt
téléphone, un telephone
télé(vision), la TV, television
température, la temperature
temps, le time; weather
   un emploi du temps schedule
   Quel temps fait-il? What's the weather like?
tennis, le tennis
   un court de tennis tennis court

une raquette de tennis tennis racquet
thé, le tea
théâtre, un theater
ticket, un ticket
timbre, un postage stamp
timide shy
toi you
toilette, une toilet
   les toilettes restroom
tomate, une tomato
ton your
total, un total
toujours always
tour, un turn (in a game)
tourne:
   Tourne à droite. Turn right.
   Tourne à gauche. Turn left.
train, un train
tranche (de pain), une slice, piece (of bread)
transport, un transportation
   moyen de transport method of transportation
travailleur(-euse) hardworking
treize thirteen
trente thirty
trente et un thirty one
très very
trois three
troisième third
trouve: se trouve is located
   Mon école se trouve à... My school is in/at . . .
   Où se trouve... ? Where is . . . ?
tu you

U

un(e) a; one
   un peu a little
université, une university, college
utile useful
   expressions utiles useful phrases

V

Va tout droit. Go straight ahead.
valise, une suitcase
vanille, la vanilla

vas: Tu vas rester combien de temps? How long are you going to stay?
vélo, un bicycle
vendredi, (le) Friday
vent, le wind
   il fait du vent it's windy
vert(e) green
vêtement, un article of clothing
viande, la meat
vie, une life, lifetime
vieille (*see* vieux)
viens: D'où viens-tu? Where do you come from?
vietnamien(ne) Vietnamese
vieux (vieille) old
ville, une town, city
vingt twenty
   quatre-vingts eighty
vingt-cinq twenty five
vingt-deux twenty two
vingt et un twenty one
vingt-huit twenty eight
vingt-neuf twenty nine
vingt-quatre twenty four
vingt-sept twenty seven
vingt-six twenty six
vingt-trois twenty three
violet(te) purple
visite, une visit
visiter to visit
vœux: Meilleurs vœux! Best wishes!
voici here is/are
voilà there is/are
vois: je vois I see
vol, un flight
   le numéro du vol the flight number
volley(-ball), le volleyball
voudrais: je voudrais I'd like
vous you
   chez vous at your house
voyage, un trip
   Bon voyage! Enjoy your trip!
voyager to travel
vrai(e) true

Y

y there

Z

zéro, un zero
zoo, un zoo